MASTERING THE TAX FREE LIVING

Unlock the Secrets to Building Wealth Without Paying More Than You Need

Andy E. Long

Legal Disclaimer

The information provided in this book, Mastering the Tax-Free Living, is for general informational purposes only and does not constitute legal, tax, financial, or professional advice. While every effort has been made to ensure the accuracy and reliability of the information, the author and publisher make no representations or warranties of any kind, express or implied, about the completeness, accuracy, reliability, suitability, or availability of the information, products, services, or related graphics contained in this book for any purpose. Any reliance you place on such information is therefore strictly at your own risk.

The strategies and suggestions provided are based on the author's research, experience, and interpretation of relevant tax laws, which are subject to change. Tax laws vary by jurisdiction, and the applicability of tax strategies can differ significantly based on individual circumstances. Readers are encouraged to consult with qualified professionals, such as certified accountants, tax advisors, or attorneys, to address their specific needs and goals.

The author and publisher disclaim any liability for errors or omissions in this book and shall not be held liable for any loss, damage, or financial hardship caused by reliance on the information contained herein. Readers are solely responsible for the decisions they make based on the contents of this book.

This book is not affiliated with or endorsed by any government agency or financial institution. References to any laws, rules, or policies are provided as examples and are not guaranteed to be current or applicable to your specific situation.

By reading this book, you agree that the author and publisher are not responsible for the success or failure of your financial decisions, and you assume full responsibility for your actions.

For personalized advice, always seek guidance from a licensed professional.

Dedication

To those who dare to dream of financial freedom
and pursue a life unbound by limitations,
this book is for you.

To my family and loved ones, whose unwavering support and encouragement have been my greatest wealth,
thank you for believing in me.

And to everyone striving to take control of their finances and build a legacy,
may this book serve as a guide and inspiration on your journey.

TABLE OF CONTENTS

Chapter 1: Introduction: Breaking Free from Financial Chains

Financial freedom is a dream many aspire to, yet for most, it feels like a mirage—visible but always just out of reach. For countless individuals, the chains of taxes, debt, and financial obligations weigh heavily, preventing them from achieving the life they envision. But what if there was a way to break free? What if you could reclaim control, not by earning more, but by keeping more of what you already have? This book isn't about avoiding responsibility or cutting corners; it's about understanding the game and finally playing it to win.

The financial system often feels like an intricate puzzle, where the rules are deliberately kept obscure. Governments and financial institutions benefit from this confusion, encouraging a mindset of compliance without comprehension. But there's an empowering truth waiting to be uncovered: those who learn the system's intricacies aren't merely participants—they become masters. It's not about dodging obligations; it's about navigating them strategically, legally, and effectively.

Taxes, for instance, are often perceived as an unavoidable drain on your earnings. Many people begrudgingly accept deductions from their income without asking questions or exploring alternatives. Yet, hidden within the complex web of tax laws are countless opportunities—opportunities designed to incentivize growth, investment, and entrepreneurship. These aren't loopholes; they're tools, and they're available to everyone who knows how to find them. What separates the wealthy from the rest isn't just their income—it's their understanding of these tools.

Consider this: the wealthiest individuals and corporations across the globe operate within the same tax systems as everyone else. They don't have secret rules or exclusive advantages. What they do have is knowledge. They understand how to structure their lives, investments, and businesses to minimize tax liabilities and maximize wealth accumulation. This isn't a privilege; it's a skill—one that anyone can learn and apply.

Breaking free from financial chains requires more than just knowledge; it demands a shift in perspective. It's about moving from a reactive approach, where money controls you, to a proactive mindset, where you take the reins. This transformation begins with questioning the narratives you've been taught about taxes, wealth, and financial planning. It involves challenging the belief that you must simply accept the status quo, and instead, adopting the mindset that every dollar has a purpose and every financial decision should work toward your long-term goals.

This book is your invitation to a financial awakening. It's a guide that bridges the gap between frustration and empowerment. Each chapter is designed to dismantle the barriers holding you back, offering practical strategies and actionable insights to help you navigate the complexities of modern finance. Whether you're just starting your journey or seeking to refine an already solid financial plan, the path to freedom begins here.

As you turn these pages, you'll gain more than just information—you'll uncover a new way of thinking, a blueprint for financial independence.

The chains of financial insecurity don't have to define your life. With the right tools and the right mindset, you can break free, step into control, and begin building the wealth and freedom you deserve. The journey starts now.

The Journey to Tax-Free Living

Every journey begins with a single step, and the path to tax-free living is no different. It's a road paved with knowledge, strategy, and a willingness to break free from conventional financial thinking. Throughout history, individuals and societies have sought ways to minimize their tax burdens, not to escape their responsibilities, but to thrive within the framework of the law. Think of entrepreneurs like Andrew Carnegie, who understood the power of reinvesting earnings into enterprises to reduce tax obligations while building vast empires. Or consider modern-day business leaders who leverage trusts, tax-deferred accounts, and charitable donations to grow their wealth and make impactful contributions.

But this isn't just a story of billionaires and moguls. It's a narrative that includes everyday people—parents saving for their children's education, retirees maximizing their nest eggs, and young professionals finding ways to make their income stretch further. For these individuals, mastering tax-free strategies means more money in their pockets to fund their dreams, whether that's traveling the world, launching a passion project, or simply enjoying peace of mind.

Tax-free living isn't about avoiding taxes; it's about understanding how to use the tools that are already available to you. The journey may seem daunting at first. After all, tax codes are notoriously complex, filled with legal jargon that feels intentionally confusing. But with guidance, this labyrinth becomes a map. It's a path you can follow step by step, learning to recognize opportunities, avoid pitfalls, and align your financial decisions with your personal goals.

Why Understanding Taxes is Key to Wealth

Taxes touch every part of your financial life, from the paycheck you earn to the investments you grow and the purchases you make. Yet, for many, they remain a mystery—a black box that drains a significant portion of their income without much thought. Understanding taxes is more than just a skill; it's a cornerstone of building sustainable wealth.

Imagine for a moment that your finances are like a leaky bucket. You can keep pouring water in—working harder, earning more—but if you don't address the leaks, your efforts are wasted. Taxes are one of the largest leaks in most people's financial buckets. The difference between those who struggle and those who thrive isn't necessarily the size of the bucket, but how well they manage the leaks.

When you understand the tax system, you unlock a level of control over your finances that few achieve. You begin to see how decisions—like buying a home, starting a business, or choosing a retirement plan—can directly influence your tax obligations. You learn to recognize the incentives built into the system, designed to reward behaviors like investing in renewable energy, saving for the future, or supporting charitable causes.

Mastering taxes doesn't just benefit you—it benefits your community and the causes you care about. By allocating your resources more effectively, you can support initiatives that align with your values while building a legacy of financial stability for yourself and your family.

Who This Book is For

This book isn't just for accountants, financial planners, or wealthy investors. It's for anyone who has ever looked at their paycheck and wondered where it all went. It's for parents trying to stretch their household budgets, entrepreneurs balancing the risks and rewards of starting a business, and retirees navigating the complexities of living on a fixed income.

If you've ever felt trapped by financial limitations, this book is for you. Perhaps you've worked hard, saved diligently, and still find yourself wondering why financial freedom seems so elusive. Or maybe you're just beginning your financial journey, eager to avoid common mistakes and set yourself up for success. Wherever you are on your path, this book offers a way forward.

You don't need a background in finance to benefit from these pages. You don't even need to know the difference between a deduction and a credit—yet. What you do need is an open mind, a willingness to learn, and the determination to take control of your financial future.

This isn't just another book filled with generic advice or cookie-cutter solutions. It's a practical guide, rooted in real-world applications and tailored to the realities of modern life. It's a roadmap for navigating the complexities of the tax system, making informed decisions, and achieving the financial freedom you deserve. Whether you're looking to reduce your tax burden, grow your wealth, or simply make smarter financial choices, this book is here to help you take the next step.

Chapter 2: Understanding the Tax System

Taxes are often regarded as one of life's greatest certainties, yet few people truly understand the system that governs them. For most, it feels like an intricate web of rules and regulations designed to confuse rather than clarify. The truth, however, is that the tax system is not an enemy to be feared—it's a structure that rewards those who take the time to learn its inner workings. Understanding the tax system isn't about mastering every line of the tax code; it's about recognizing the opportunities it provides and using them to your advantage.

At its core, taxation is about the relationship between individuals, businesses, and the government. Taxes fund essential public services, infrastructure, and programs that benefit society. Yet within this system lies a carefully designed series of incentives. These incentives are not arbitrary; they exist to guide economic behavior, encouraging actions that align with broader societal goals. Whether it's investing in renewable energy, saving for retirement, or supporting local businesses, these incentives are built into the fabric of the tax system, waiting for those who know where to look.

For most people, the idea of reducing taxes seems reserved for the wealthy or the highly educated. But this misconception is far from the truth. The tax code doesn't play favorites—it's accessible to anyone willing to understand its language. For example, many individuals miss out on significant deductions simply because they don't know they exist. From health savings accounts to education credits, the system is filled with opportunities that can ease your financial burden if you know how to claim them.

One of the most critical steps in understanding the tax system is to shift your perspective. Taxes are not merely an annual obligation to be endured; they are a year-round component of your financial strategy. Every decision, from the way you earn your income to how you choose to spend or save it, has tax implications. By approaching taxes as a part of your overall financial planning, you can begin to make choices that align with your goals and reduce unnecessary liabilities.

Take, for instance, the difference between earned and passive income. Many people work tirelessly in jobs that are taxed at the highest rates, unaware that alternative income streams—such as investments or rental properties—offer significantly lower tax burdens. Similarly, entrepreneurs and small business owners often overlook the numerous deductions and credits available to them, leaving money on the table that could otherwise fuel growth or stability.

Understanding the tax system also means recognizing its global implications. In a world where borders are increasingly irrelevant to commerce and lifestyle, tax laws vary widely from one country to another. For those willing to explore options beyond their home country, there are opportunities to minimize taxes legally by leveraging international tax treaties or relocating to tax-favorable jurisdictions.

This chapter isn't about turning you into a tax professional; it's about equipping you with the foundational knowledge to approach taxes with confidence. When you understand the system, you move from being a passive participant to an active strategist. The tax system, once a source of frustration, becomes a tool that works in your favor. And with the right strategies, it can be one of the most powerful assets on your journey toward financial independence.

How Taxes Impact Your Wealth

Every dollar you earn, spend, or save interacts with the tax system in some way, often determining how much of your wealth you get to keep. Taxes are not just about the amount deducted from your paycheck—they extend to how your investments grow, the equity you build in a home, and even the legacy you leave behind. Understanding how taxes affect wealth is a critical step toward financial control.

For starters, income taxes are often the most visible form of taxation. Whether you're an employee, a freelancer, or a business owner, the way you earn money determines how heavily it is taxed. For example, traditional salaried income is taxed at progressively higher rates as your earnings increase. On the other hand, capital gains, derived from investments like stocks or real estate, are taxed at lower rates, especially if they are held for the long term. Recognizing this difference allows you to make decisions that can significantly alter your financial trajectory.

Then there are payroll taxes, often misunderstood as mere deductions for Social Security and Medicare. While these taxes provide essential services, they disproportionately affect those who rely solely on wages for income. By diversifying income sources, such as through passive investments or rental properties, you can reduce this burden.

Local, state, and federal taxes also play a significant role. Federal taxes set the baseline, but state and local taxes vary widely, creating opportunities for strategic planning. Living in a state with no income tax, for instance, can result in significant savings over time. However, these savings might be offset by higher property or sales taxes, requiring a balanced understanding of the total tax picture.

Taxes don't just subtract from your wealth—they can also influence how it grows. Retirement accounts like 401(k)s and IRAs offer tax advantages, either by deferring taxes or allowing earnings to grow tax-free. Similarly, health savings accounts (HSAs) provide a triple tax benefit: contributions, growth, and withdrawals for qualified expenses are all tax-free. Knowing how to use these tools can mean the difference between a comfortable retirement and financial insecurity.

The Legal Framework: What You Need to Know

The tax system may seem daunting, but at its core, it operates within a clear legal framework. Understanding the structure of this framework demystifies taxes and empowers you to make informed choices.

The Internal Revenue Code (IRC) is the foundation of tax law in the United States, outlining how taxes are assessed, collected, and enforced. While the code itself is vast and complex, its purpose is to provide a standardized system for taxation. This system is complemented by state and local regulations, which add layers of complexity but also opportunities for savings.

Key legal concepts like deductions, credits, and exemptions are essential to navigate. Deductions reduce your taxable income, lowering the amount you owe. Credits, on the other hand, directly reduce your tax bill, often dollar-for-dollar. Exemptions, though limited in recent tax reforms, provide targeted relief for specific situations, such as dependents or charitable donations.

Another critical aspect is tax compliance. Filing taxes accurately and on time is not just a legal obligation but also an opportunity to maximize benefits. Tax software and professional services can help, but understanding the basics ensures that you're not leaving money on the table.

Audits are often feared but are relatively rare and usually triggered by discrepancies or red flags. Keeping thorough records of income, expenses, and deductions protects you from undue scrutiny. The IRS is not out to punish taxpayers but to ensure compliance with the law, and staying informed helps you navigate this process confidently.

Myths and Misconceptions About Taxes

Many people approach taxes with a mix of dread and misinformation, leading to costly mistakes. Busting these myths is crucial for gaining clarity and confidence in managing your finances.

One common myth is that only the wealthy benefit from tax breaks. In reality, the tax code includes numerous provisions designed for the average taxpayer. For instance, tax credits for education, homeownership, and childcare are widely available and can significantly reduce your tax burden.

Another misconception is that tax refunds are a financial windfall. In truth, receiving a large refund often means you've overpaid taxes throughout the year. Adjusting your withholdings can put that money back in your pocket sooner, allowing you to invest or pay off debt instead of giving the government an interest-free loan.

There's also the belief that filing taxes is too complicated to do without professional help. While complex situations may require expert guidance, most individuals can handle their taxes with the right tools and resources. Free filing options, IRS guides, and online calculators make the process more accessible than ever.

Some fear that claiming deductions or credits increases the likelihood of an audit. While accuracy is essential, taking advantage of legal tax benefits does not automatically raise red flags. Audits are generally triggered by inconsistencies or unusually large claims, not by the use of legitimate tax-saving strategies.

Finally, many assume that tax planning is only relevant during tax season. In reality, the most effective strategies are implemented year-round. Whether it's adjusting retirement contributions, tracking expenses, or exploring new income opportunities, proactive planning ensures you're prepared long before deadlines loom.

By dispelling these myths, you can approach taxes with a clearer understanding and greater confidence, transforming what once felt like an overwhelming obligation into a powerful tool for building wealth.

Chapter 3: Tax-Free Income Sources

Earning an income feels like a victory until you watch a significant chunk of it disappear into taxes. For many, the idea of keeping more of what they earn seems like a distant dream, reserved only for the well-connected or financially elite. But there's good news: tax-free income isn't just a concept for the few—it's an achievable reality for anyone willing to explore the options available. This isn't about loopholes or bending rules; it's about recognizing the opportunities that exist and leveraging them strategically to create a stronger financial future.

Tax-free income sources come in many forms, and each has the potential to shift the way you think about earning and saving money. One of the most widely known yet underutilized options is the Roth IRA. Contributions to this retirement account are made with after-tax dollars, but the beauty lies in what comes next: every dollar of growth and every withdrawal during retirement is completely tax-free. For those who start early and let compounding work its magic, this can result in substantial savings.

Another avenue for tax-free income lies in municipal bonds. These are essentially loans you provide to state or local governments in exchange for interest payments. The catch? That interest is often exempt from federal taxes and, in many cases, state and local taxes as well. While the returns may not match riskier investments like stocks, the security and tax benefits make them a worthwhile addition to a diversified portfolio.

Health savings accounts (HSAs) are another gem, offering a triple tax advantage that few other tools can match. Contributions are tax-deductible, growth within the account is tax-free, and withdrawals for qualified medical expenses are also tax-free. For those with high-deductible health plans, an HSA can serve as both a short-term health fund and a long-term tax-free investment vehicle.

Life insurance policies, particularly those with cash value components, also offer unique opportunities. While the primary purpose of life insurance is to provide for loved ones after your passing, some policies allow you to borrow against the cash value without triggering taxable events.

This can be a valuable resource during retirement or when unexpected expenses arise.

And then there are personal strategies, such as leveraging the sale of your primary residence. If you meet the residency requirements, profits from the sale of your home—up to $250,000 for individuals and $500,000 for married couples—can be completely tax-free. This can be a game-changer for those looking to downsize or relocate.

The idea of tax-free income isn't about evasion or secrecy; it's about aligning your financial goals with tools designed to help you succeed. By incorporating these sources into your overall strategy, you're not just reducing your tax burden—you're empowering yourself to grow and sustain wealth in ways that support your aspirations. As you uncover these options, you'll start to see how keeping more of what you earn can transform not just your finances but your entire perspective on what's possible. Let this chapter be your guide to tapping into the hidden potential of tax-free income and unlocking opportunities you never knew existed.

Leveraging Tax-Advantaged Accounts

Tax-advantaged accounts are often viewed as tools for the distant future, but their benefits extend far beyond just retirement planning. They represent some of the most powerful and accessible ways to create income that avoids heavy taxation. The key lies in understanding how each type of account works and aligning it with your financial goals.

Take Roth IRAs, for example. Unlike traditional IRAs, Roth accounts are funded with after-tax dollars, meaning you don't get an immediate tax deduction. However, the trade-off is worth it: all earnings grow tax-free, and withdrawals during retirement are completely untaxed, provided you follow the rules. This makes the Roth IRA an excellent option for individuals who expect to be in a higher tax bracket in the future or those who want to minimize tax burdens in retirement.

Another lesser-known but highly effective tool is the Health Savings Account (HSA). Often overshadowed by other investment vehicles, the HSA is a triple-tax-advantaged account.

Contributions are deductible, earnings grow tax-free, and withdrawals for qualified medical expenses are untaxed. What many people overlook is that HSAs can also serve as a stealth retirement account. If you don't use the funds for medical expenses, you can withdraw them for any purpose after age 65, with the only downside being regular income tax—essentially converting it into a tax-deferred account with unparalleled flexibility.

Don't forget about employer-sponsored plans like 401(k)s. While contributions to a traditional 401(k) reduce taxable income in the present, Roth 401(k)s combine the immediate ease of payroll deductions with the future tax-free benefits of a Roth IRA. Employers often match contributions up to a certain percentage, providing an instant return on investment that can't be ignored.

The real power of these accounts lies in consistency. A 25-year-old contributing the maximum annual amount to a Roth IRA could see their investment grow into a tax-free nest egg of nearly $2 million by age 65, assuming an average annual return of 7%. This isn't theoretical; countless retirees today enjoy financial security because they started early and stayed committed.

Income Streams That Escape Taxation

Some income streams aren't just tax-efficient—they're completely tax-free. These are the hidden gems of the financial world, often overlooked because they require a shift in mindset or a bit of research to uncover.

One prime example is municipal bond interest. When you purchase a municipal bond, you're essentially lending money to a state or local government. In return, you receive interest payments, which are typically exempt from federal taxes and, in many cases, state and local taxes if you live in the issuing state. These bonds are especially attractive to individuals in higher tax brackets, as the tax savings amplify their effective returns.

Another source of untaxed income is the profit from selling your primary residence, provided you meet the requirements. If you've lived in your home for at least two out of the last five years before selling, you can exclude up to $250,000 of capital gains ($500,000 for married couples) from taxation. This exclusion can be a game-changer, allowing homeowners to leverage rising real estate values without a tax penalty.

Certain scholarships and grants also fall into this category. For students or parents saving for college, education-related income like scholarships, fellowships, and grants used for qualified expenses often escape taxation entirely. Leveraging these options reduces the financial strain of education and keeps more money in your pocket.

For business owners, income streams can be optimized through tools like Qualified Small Business Stock (QSBS), which allows for significant tax exclusions on gains if the stock is held for at least five years. Entrepreneurs building companies from the ground up should explore this option as part of their long-term strategy.

Smart Investments for Tax-Free Earnings

Investments are one of the best ways to grow wealth, and certain vehicles allow you to do so without the drag of taxes. Choosing the right options can mean the difference between average results and extraordinary outcomes.

For those looking for predictable returns, U.S. Treasury securities, such as Series EE and I savings bonds, provide interest that is exempt from state and local taxes. These instruments are not only safe but also offer unique tax advantages when used for education expenses.

Real estate investments structured within a self-directed IRA can also yield substantial tax-free benefits. By purchasing properties through an IRA, you can grow rental income or flip properties without triggering immediate taxes. While this strategy requires a hands-on approach and adherence to strict rules, the long-term benefits can be substantial.

Additionally, permanent life insurance policies with cash value components allow policyholders to grow wealth tax-free. Over time, you can borrow against the accumulated cash value without triggering a taxable event. This strategy is particularly useful for those seeking liquidity without dipping into taxable investments.

For investors seeking exposure to the stock market, tax-free growth is achievable through strategies like buying and holding. Capital gains aren't realized until the asset is sold, meaning your wealth can grow uninterrupted for decades. Pairing this approach with tax-advantaged accounts amplifies its effectiveness, creating a double-layered shield against unnecessary taxes.

The beauty of tax-free income strategies is that they're accessible to anyone willing to explore their options. These aren't shortcuts—they're tools designed to reward informed, strategic decision-making. By leveraging these opportunities, you not only reduce the tax burden on your current earnings but also set the stage for a more secure, prosperous financial future.

Chapter 4: The Power of Tax-Efficient Investing

Investing is often seen as the ultimate tool for building wealth, but what many people overlook is the crucial role taxes play in shaping those returns. It's not just about how much your investments grow—it's about how much you get to keep. Tax-efficient investing isn't just a strategy for the wealthy; it's a transformative approach that anyone can adopt to make their money work harder and smarter. When you understand how to minimize taxes on your investments, you're unlocking a hidden layer of potential that can dramatically accelerate your journey to financial independence.

The first step to mastering tax-efficient investing is recognizing that not all investment gains are created equal. Dividends, interest, capital gains, and rental income are taxed differently, depending on where and how they're earned. For example, long-term capital gains, which come from holding an asset for more than a year, are taxed at a lower rate than short-term gains, which are treated as ordinary income. Knowing this distinction is critical for timing your trades and holding assets strategically.

Tax-advantaged accounts are another cornerstone of tax-efficient investing. Accounts like Roth IRAs, 401(k)s, and Health Savings Accounts provide unique opportunities to grow wealth without the drag of taxes. Roth accounts are particularly powerful because they allow your investments to grow tax-free forever, and withdrawals in retirement come with no strings attached. Meanwhile, traditional IRAs and 401(k)s defer taxes, letting your money compound faster. The magic of compounding becomes even more impressive when it's free from the erosion of annual tax bills.

But tax efficiency isn't limited to retirement accounts. Where you hold your investments—known as asset location—matters just as much as what you invest in. Tax-efficient assets, such as index funds and municipal bonds, are better suited for taxable accounts because they generate less taxable income. On the other hand, assets with higher turnover or significant distributions, like actively managed funds or high-yield bonds, should be placed in tax-advantaged accounts to shield their income from immediate taxation.

For those investing in real estate, strategies like depreciation and 1031 exchanges offer powerful ways to defer or eliminate taxes. Depreciation allows you to offset rental income by deducting a property's wear and tear, while a 1031 exchange lets you defer capital gains taxes by reinvesting proceeds from a property sale into a similar investment. These tools aren't just for seasoned investors—they're accessible to anyone willing to learn the rules and apply them effectively.

Tax-efficient investing also requires looking ahead. Tax-loss harvesting, for example, is a strategy that involves selling underperforming investments to offset gains elsewhere in your portfolio. This not only reduces your tax bill but also provides an opportunity to rebalance and reinvest in assets with stronger potential. Similarly, timing your withdrawals in retirement can help you avoid bumping into higher tax brackets, ensuring that your hard-earned money lasts longer.

The beauty of tax-efficient investing is its scalability. Whether you're starting with a modest portfolio or managing substantial wealth, these strategies can be tailored to fit your situation. More importantly, they shift the focus from chasing risky, high-return investments to optimizing what you already have. It's not about taking bigger risks—it's about making smarter choices.

By embracing tax-efficient investing, you're not just enhancing your returns—you're reclaiming control over your financial future. The money you save in taxes can be reinvested, accelerating your progress toward your goals. Investing is about building security, freedom, and the life you envision for yourself and your loved ones. When taxes are no longer an obstacle, the possibilities become endless.

Tax-Deferred vs. Tax-Free Accounts

Understanding the difference between tax-deferred and tax-free accounts is the foundation of tax-efficient investing. These two types of accounts operate on different principles, and knowing when to use each can make a significant difference in your financial outcomes.

Tax-deferred accounts, such as traditional 401(k)s, IRAs, and annuities, allow you to postpone paying taxes on your contributions and investment earnings until you withdraw the money, usually in retirement. This delay can be a powerful tool because it lets your investments compound faster, without the annual erosion caused by taxes. For example, if you contribute $10,000 to a tax-deferred account and it grows to $100,000 over 20 years, you'll only pay taxes when you begin withdrawing, potentially at a lower tax rate if your income decreases in retirement.

The primary advantage of tax-deferred accounts is their immediate benefit to your current cash flow. Contributions are often deductible, meaning you lower your taxable income in the year you make them. For someone in a high tax bracket, this can provide significant savings. However, the trade-off is that withdrawals are taxed as ordinary income, and if you withdraw before age 59½, you may face additional penalties.

Tax-free accounts, on the other hand, take a different approach. With accounts like Roth IRAs, Roth 401(k)s, and health savings accounts (HSAs), you pay taxes upfront on your contributions. Once the money is in the account, however, it grows tax-free, and qualified withdrawals are completely untaxed. This is particularly advantageous if you expect to be in a higher tax bracket in the future or want to avoid taxes on investment gains entirely.

For example, contributing $6,000 annually to a Roth IRA starting at age 30 can result in a tax-free balance of over $500,000 by retirement, assuming average market returns. This is money you can use without worrying about tax implications, providing immense flexibility in managing your retirement income.

The key to leveraging these accounts effectively is to understand your current financial situation and future goals. Younger individuals or those in lower tax brackets often benefit from tax-free accounts, while high earners may find tax-deferred accounts more advantageous initially. A balanced strategy often involves using both, ensuring you have flexibility and tax efficiency at different stages of life.

Choosing the Right Investment Vehicles

Choosing the right investment vehicles within these accounts is just as important as selecting the accounts themselves. Different types of investments are taxed differently, and aligning your assets with the right accounts can save you significant amounts over time.

Tax-efficient investments for taxable accounts include municipal bonds, low-turnover index funds, and exchange-traded funds (ETFs). These generate minimal taxable income, making them ideal for accounts where gains are taxed annually. Municipal bonds, for instance, provide interest income that is often exempt from federal taxes and sometimes from state taxes as well. Index funds and ETFs typically have lower turnover, meaning fewer taxable events like capital gains distributions.

In tax-deferred or tax-free accounts, high-yield investments and actively managed funds are more appropriate. These assets often generate substantial income or frequent taxable events, which are shielded within the account. For example, placing a dividend-paying stock in a Roth IRA allows you to reinvest dividends without worrying about taxes, maximizing compounding over time.

A beginner-friendly approach to building a tax-efficient portfolio involves three steps:
1. **Assess your goals:** Are you focused on long-term growth, current income, or a combination? Your objectives will determine which accounts and investments are most suitable.
2. **Allocate assets strategically:** Divide your investments across accounts based on their tax characteristics. Tax-efficient assets like index funds go in taxable accounts, while tax-inefficient assets like REITs or actively managed funds go in tax-advantaged accounts.
3. **Rebalance periodically:** Over time, your portfolio's allocation may shift due to market fluctuations. Regular rebalancing ensures you stay aligned with your goals while taking advantage of tax-saving opportunities like tax-loss harvesting in taxable accounts.

While tax-efficient investing requires planning, the rewards are well worth the effort. By selecting the right mix of accounts and investments, you can minimize tax drag, maximize growth, and create a portfolio that supports your long-term financial aspirations. This isn't about chasing trends or taking excessive risks—it's about making thoughtful decisions that compound over time, allowing you to achieve financial independence with confidence and control.

Strategies for Long-Term Growth

Building wealth over the long term is not about chasing quick returns or timing the market—it's about consistent, strategic investing with a focus on efficiency. Tax-efficient investing amplifies growth by minimizing unnecessary losses to taxes, allowing compounding to work uninterrupted over time. Developing a clear strategy for long-term growth ensures that your investments not only grow but also retain the maximum value when it matters most.

One of the most impactful strategies for long-term growth is to prioritize tax-advantaged accounts. Accounts like Roth IRAs, Roth 401(k)s, and Health Savings Accounts (HSAs) provide the ideal foundation for growth because they shelter investments from the erosion of taxes. In a Roth IRA, for instance, every dollar of growth remains untouched by taxes, meaning the full power of compounding is harnessed. For someone starting at age 30 and contributing $6,500 annually, the account could grow to over $1 million by retirement, completely tax-free.

Beyond choosing the right accounts, asset allocation plays a critical role in long-term growth. Diversification across asset classes—such as stocks, bonds, and real estate—helps to balance risk while maximizing returns. Equities, particularly in the form of low-cost index funds or exchange-traded funds (ETFs), are often the cornerstone of a growth-focused portfolio. These investments provide exposure to the market's upward trajectory over time while keeping costs low. Pairing this with tax-efficient vehicles ensures that capital gains and dividends are either deferred or eliminated, depending on the account type.

For those seeking to incorporate fixed-income investments, municipal bonds are a standout choice. These bonds not only provide stable income but often come with the added benefit of being exempt from federal taxes—and sometimes state and local taxes as well. This makes them an excellent option for high-income individuals looking for a conservative investment that doesn't compromise tax efficiency.

Another strategy for long-term growth involves reinvesting earnings. Dividend reinvestment plans (DRIPs) allow investors to automatically reinvest dividends into additional shares, avoiding the tax drag that comes with cashing out dividends in a taxable account. When used in a tax-advantaged account, this reinvestment compounds tax-free, accelerating growth over time.

Tax-loss harvesting is a more active strategy that can also support long-term growth by reducing your tax liability. This involves selling investments that have declined in value to offset gains from other assets or income. The funds from the sale can be reinvested in similar assets, maintaining the portfolio's structure while creating tax savings. Over decades, this can amount to significant retained value.

Timing also plays a pivotal role in a long-term strategy. For tax-deferred accounts like traditional 401(k)s or IRAs, withdrawals in retirement should be carefully planned to avoid unnecessary taxes. By withdrawing funds strategically—often in years where taxable income is lower—you can minimize the impact on your overall wealth.

Finally, the concept of tax diversification deserves attention. Just as asset diversification spreads risk across investments, tax diversification spreads risk across different tax treatments. By balancing contributions between tax-deferred, tax-free, and taxable accounts, you create flexibility in managing your wealth throughout life. This ensures that no matter how tax laws or personal circumstances change, you have options for minimizing your liability.

These strategies are not about quick wins—they're about building a robust plan that stands the test of time. Long-term growth requires patience, discipline, and an understanding of how to make every financial decision work in your favor. The combination of tax-efficient accounts, smart asset selection, and strategic management provides a clear path to sustained financial independence. With these tools at your disposal, your investments can grow into a legacy of wealth and stability for generations to come.

Chapter 5. Real Estate and Tax-Free Wealth

Real estate has long been regarded as one of the most reliable avenues for building wealth, and it's no secret why. Unlike many other investments, real estate offers tangible assets, predictable income potential, and, perhaps most importantly, powerful tax advantages. What many people don't realize is just how much the tax code favors real estate investors. By understanding the unique benefits of this asset class, you can transform your investment strategy into a wealth-building machine that not only generates income but also shields it from unnecessary taxation.

One of the most appealing aspects of real estate is the capital gains exclusion on the sale of a primary residence. If you've owned and lived in your home for at least two out of the last five years, you can exclude up to $250,000 of profit ($500,000 for married couples) from taxes. For many homeowners, this represents one of the largest tax-free income opportunities they'll ever encounter. Whether you're upgrading to a larger home, downsizing for retirement, or simply cashing in on a hot housing market, this exclusion allows you to pocket substantial gains without worrying about a tax bill.

For those venturing into rental properties, the benefits multiply. Rental income is a steady cash flow that's often underestimated in its tax efficiency. While the income itself is taxable, real estate investors can offset a significant portion of their earnings through deductions. Expenses such as property management fees, repairs, insurance, and even travel to maintain the property can be written off, reducing your taxable income. One of the most powerful deductions available to landlords is depreciation. The IRS allows you to deduct a portion of your property's value each year as it "wears out," even though the property itself may actually be appreciating in market value.

Real estate investors also have access to the 1031 exchange, a game-changing tool for deferring taxes. Named after Section 1031 of the tax code, this strategy allows you to sell one investment property and reinvest the proceeds into another "like-kind" property without paying capital gains taxes. This means you can continue to build your portfolio, moving into higher-value properties and increasing your cash flow, all while deferring taxes indefinitely. The benefits compound over time, making the 1031 exchange one of the most effective ways to grow wealth in real estate.

Even beyond these tax advantages, real estate provides unique opportunities to generate income through short-term rentals, house hacking, or commercial leasing. Short-term rentals, popularized by platforms like Airbnb, can yield significantly higher returns than traditional leasing if managed effectively. House hacking, where you live in one unit of a multi-family property while renting out the others, allows you to cover your mortgage and live nearly expense-free. These strategies not only boost income but also create pathways for financial independence with minimal tax burdens.

What sets real estate apart is its accessibility. You don’t need to be a millionaire to get started. With options like FHA loans requiring as little as 3.5% down, or partnerships that split ownership costs, entering the real estate market is more achievable than most realize. The key is understanding the opportunities and leveraging the tax benefits to maximize returns.

Real estate isn't just about owning property—it's about building a legacy. The tax advantages baked into real estate investing allow you to grow your wealth in ways that few other assets can match. By combining strategic planning, smart financing, and an awareness of the tax benefits available, you can turn real estate into a powerful engine for creating and preserving tax-free wealth. This is more than an investment—it's a path to financial freedom and security for generations to come.

Capitalizing on Real Estate Exemptions

Real estate is unique among investments in that it offers a range of exemptions and benefits specifically designed to reduce tax burdens. One of the most powerful tools at your disposal is the capital gains tax exemption on the sale of your primary residence. If you've lived in your home for at least two of the last five years, you can exclude up to $250,000 of profit from taxation as a single filer, or $500,000 if you're married and filing jointly. This exemption allows homeowners to benefit from the appreciation of their property without handing over a large portion of their earnings to the IRS.

For example, imagine buying a home for $300,000 and selling it five years later for $500,000. Under normal circumstances, the $200,000 gain would be subject to capital gains tax. However, if you qualify for the exemption, that entire amount can remain tax-free, providing a substantial boost to your financial standing. What's more, this exemption isn't a one-time deal—it can be used repeatedly, provided you meet the residency requirements. This makes homeownership not only a pathway to building wealth but also a tax-advantaged strategy for reinvesting in new opportunities.

Another underutilized exemption involves rolling gains into a 1031 exchange. While typically associated with investment properties, the 1031 exchange can also be used in creative ways by savvy investors who convert a primary residence into a rental property before selling. By renting out the property and adhering to specific rules, you can defer taxes on gains and reinvest them into another property, continuing to grow your portfolio without the immediate tax burden.

Real estate exemptions also extend to property taxes in certain cases. Many states offer homestead exemptions, which reduce the taxable value of your home and lower your annual property tax bill. These exemptions are often available to senior citizens, veterans, or individuals with disabilities, but even general homeowners may qualify depending on their state's rules. Checking with your local assessor's office can reveal savings opportunities you might otherwise overlook.

Tax-Free Benefits of Homeownership

Homeownership is often celebrated as a cornerstone of financial stability, and for good reason—it provides not just a place to live but also an array of tax advantages that can significantly reduce your overall liabilities. Perhaps the most well-known benefit is the ability to deduct mortgage interest from your taxable income. For homeowners with substantial mortgages, this deduction can save thousands of dollars each year, particularly in the early stages of the loan when interest payments are at their highest.

In addition to mortgage interest, property taxes are also deductible, further reducing the financial burden of owning a home. While recent changes to the tax code have capped the combined deduction for state and local taxes at $10,000, this benefit remains valuable, especially in high-cost areas where property taxes can be a significant expense.

Energy-efficient home improvements provide another opportunity for tax-free benefits. Federal and state programs often offer credits or deductions for installing solar panels, upgrading to energy-efficient windows, or improving insulation. These incentives not only reduce your upfront costs but also lower your utility bills, creating long-term savings that compound over time.

For those looking to maximize the financial benefits of homeownership, renting out part of your property can provide tax-free income under certain circumstances. The IRS allows you to rent your home for up to 14 days per year without reporting the income, regardless of the amount you charge. This is particularly useful for homeowners in popular vacation destinations or near major events, where short-term rental rates can be substantial.

Beyond these specific deductions and credits, homeownership offers intangible benefits that indirectly support wealth building. Owning property provides stability, reduces housing costs over the long term, and allows you to build equity instead of paying rent to a landlord. That equity can then be leveraged through home equity loans or lines of credit, providing tax-advantaged borrowing options for renovations, investments, or other financial needs.

When approached strategically, homeownership becomes more than just a milestone—it's a powerful tool for creating and preserving wealth. By understanding and utilizing the tax benefits available, homeowners can significantly enhance their financial position while enjoying the stability and freedom that comes with owning their property. Real estate, when managed wisely, serves as both a home and a foundation for lasting prosperity.

Real Estate Investment Trusts (REITs)

Real estate investment trusts, or REITs, are an exceptional way for individuals to access the benefits of real estate investing without the challenges and responsibilities of property ownership. These publicly traded companies pool resources to invest in, operate, or finance income-generating real estate, allowing everyday investors to own a piece of high-value assets such as office buildings, shopping centers, apartments, and even data centers. For those looking to diversify their portfolio and leverage the tax advantages of real estate without direct management, REITs offer a compelling solution.

One of the most attractive features of REITs is their ability to generate regular income. By law, REITs are required to distribute at least 90% of their taxable income to shareholders in the form of dividends. This makes them a reliable source of passive income for investors, particularly those in or nearing retirement. Unlike traditional rental properties, REITs remove the stress of dealing with tenants, repairs, or property maintenance while still providing consistent returns.

From a tax perspective, REIT dividends offer a unique set of advantages. While they are generally taxed as ordinary income, recent tax reforms have introduced a qualified business income (QBI) deduction for REIT dividends. This allows investors to deduct up to 20% of their REIT dividend income, effectively lowering their tax liability and increasing the net return on their investment. For example, if you receive $10,000 in REIT dividends, you may only need to pay taxes on $8,000, depending on your income bracket and specific circumstances.

REITs also simplify tax reporting compared to direct property investments. Shareholders typically receive a Form 1099-DIV at the end of the year, detailing their taxable income and any return of capital, which can reduce their cost basis in the investment. This streamlined reporting process eliminates the need to track complex expenses or depreciation schedules, making REITs an appealing choice for investors who want simplicity without sacrificing returns.

Another key benefit of REITs is their liquidity. Unlike physical properties, which can take months or even years to sell, REIT shares can be bought and sold on stock exchanges just like any other publicly traded security. This provides unparalleled flexibility, allowing investors to adjust their portfolios quickly in response to changing market conditions or personal financial needs.

For investors looking to maximize the tax efficiency of their REIT holdings, combining them with tax-advantaged accounts such as IRAs or 401(k)s is an excellent strategy. By holding REITs in a Roth IRA, for instance, you can enjoy tax-free growth on your investment and withdraw dividends tax-free in retirement. This pairing magnifies the already impressive benefits of REITs, creating a powerful tool for long-term wealth accumulation.

While REITs offer many advantages, it's important to choose the right type of REIT for your financial goals. Equity REITs focus on owning and operating properties, providing income through rents and property appreciation. Mortgage REITs, on the other hand, invest in real estate debt, earning income from interest payments. Hybrid

REITs combine both approaches, offering a mix of income streams. Understanding the differences allows you to align your investments with your risk tolerance and income expectations.

Real estate investment trusts democratize access to the lucrative world of real estate, making it possible for anyone with a brokerage account to participate. They offer a scalable, tax-advantaged, and hassle-free way to diversify your portfolio while enjoying the stability and growth potential of real estate. For individuals seeking to build wealth without the complications of direct property management, REITs provide a practical and rewarding pathway to financial success.

Chapter 6: Entrepreneurship and Tax-Free Opportunities

Entrepreneurship has always been a cornerstone of innovation and wealth creation, offering individuals the freedom to shape their own destinies while building something meaningful. But what sets entrepreneurs apart isn't just their drive or creativity—it's their ability to leverage opportunities that others overlook. One of the most underappreciated aspects of entrepreneurship is the array of tax benefits it unlocks. By understanding and utilizing these opportunities, business owners can reduce their tax burdens, reinvest in growth, and ultimately keep more of what they earn.

When you transition from being an employee to running your own business, the tax landscape changes dramatically in your favor. As an entrepreneur, you gain access to deductions, credits, and tax-advantaged strategies that are simply unavailable to traditional workers. Expenses that were once personal—like a portion of your rent, utilities, or even your car—can now become legitimate business deductions, provided they are used for your enterprise. For instance, if you operate your business from a dedicated space in your home, you can take advantage of the home office deduction. This allows you to write off a percentage of your rent or mortgage, property taxes, and utilities based on the square footage of your office.

Another significant advantage lies in the ability to deduct startup costs. Whether you're purchasing equipment, creating a website, or hiring professional services, these initial expenses can be deducted, reducing the financial strain of launching your venture. Additionally, ongoing business expenses like travel, marketing, and employee salaries are fully deductible, providing entrepreneurs with a unique opportunity to lower taxable income while building their brand.

Entrepreneurs also gain access to retirement savings vehicles that offer substantial tax advantages. Plans like the SEP IRA, SIMPLE IRA, and Solo 401(k) allow business owners to contribute significantly higher amounts than traditional IRAs or 401(k)s for employees. These contributions are tax-deferred, meaning they reduce your current taxable income while growing tax-free until withdrawal. For instance, a Solo 401(k) enables you to contribute both as an employer and employee, potentially sheltering tens of thousands of dollars annually from taxation.

Health savings accounts (HSAs) offer another layer of tax-free opportunities for entrepreneurs. If you have a high-deductible health plan, contributions to an HSA are deductible, grow tax-free, and can be withdrawn tax-free for qualified medical expenses. This triple tax advantage is particularly valuable for entrepreneurs, who often face higher healthcare costs without the safety net of employer-sponsored insurance.

One of the most powerful tools in the entrepreneurial tax toolkit is the ability to structure your business in a way that minimizes taxes. Choosing the right entity—whether it's a sole proprietorship, LLC, S corporation, or C corporation—has profound implications for how your income is taxed. For example, S corporations allow business owners to pay themselves a reasonable salary while distributing remaining profits as dividends, which are taxed at a lower rate. Similarly, LLCs offer flexibility in how income is reported and taxed, making them a popular choice for small businesses.

Perhaps the most exciting aspect of entrepreneurship is the potential for long-term wealth creation through equity. If you build a scalable business and eventually sell it, provisions like Section 1202 of the tax code, which governs Qualified Small Business Stock (QSBS), can exclude a significant portion of your capital gains from taxation. This makes entrepreneurship not just a vehicle for earning income but also for building generational wealth.

At its core, entrepreneurship is about taking control—of your time, your resources, and your financial future. The tax benefits are not just perks; they're tools that empower business owners to grow, innovate, and succeed. By fully embracing the opportunities available, entrepreneurs can create more than just profitable businesses—they can build lives of financial freedom and lasting impact. The rewards of entrepreneurship go far beyond profits; they're about maximizing potential, both personally and professionally. And in doing so, entrepreneurs not only create opportunities for themselves but also contribute to the economy and the communities they serve.

Starting a Business with Tax Advantages

Starting a business does more than allow you to pursue your passion—it also opens the door to a world of tax advantages that can significantly reduce your financial burdens and increase your long-term wealth. As a business owner, you gain access to deductions, credits, and strategic opportunities that simply aren't available to employees. The tax code is structured to incentivize entrepreneurship, rewarding those who take the risk of starting and running a business with tools to minimize taxable income and reinvest in growth. Understanding and leveraging these advantages can transform your business from a source of income into a vehicle for financial freedom.

One of the most immediate benefits of starting a business is the ability to deduct expenses directly related to your operations. From the moment you begin planning your venture, many of your expenditures qualify as deductible startup costs. These include market research, professional services like legal and accounting fees, advertising, and even travel expenses for scouting potential locations or attending industry events. Startup costs up to $5,000 can often be deducted in the first year, with additional expenses amortized over several years, reducing your taxable income during those critical early stages.

As your business begins to generate revenue, the range of deductible expenses expands. Operational costs such as rent, utilities, employee wages, and supplies are all deductible, lowering your taxable income and freeing up cash for reinvestment. If you work from home, the home office deduction allows you to write off a portion of your rent or mortgage, utilities, and even internet expenses. The key to maximizing these deductions is meticulous record-keeping. By tracking every eligible expense, you ensure you're claiming the full range of benefits the tax code offers.

Structuring your business correctly is another critical factor in optimizing tax advantages. The type of entity you choose—whether a sole proprietorship, partnership, LLC, S corporation, or C corporation—determines how your income is taxed and what deductions you can claim. For instance, LLCs provide flexibility in how profits are reported, allowing business owners to choose between being taxed as a sole proprietor or as a corporation. S corporations are particularly popular for small businesses because they allow owners to pay themselves a reasonable salary and take the remaining profits as distributions, which are often taxed at a lower rate.

Health benefits also offer significant tax advantages for business owners. Establishing a Health Reimbursement Arrangement (HRA) or providing insurance coverage for employees allows you to deduct premiums and other medical expenses. For sole proprietors, health insurance premiums for yourself and your family are deductible, further reducing your taxable income.

Consider the case of Angela, a freelance graphic designer who transitioned her side hustle into a full-time business. By forming an LLC taxed as an S corporation, she was able to pay herself a salary while distributing additional profits at a lower tax rate. Angela also claimed the home office deduction, writing off part of her rent, and set up a Solo 401(k), allowing her to defer significant income while planning for retirement. These strategies saved her thousands of dollars in taxes annually, which she reinvested in new equipment and marketing to grow her business.

Tax credits are another area where business owners can benefit significantly. Unlike deductions, which reduce taxable income, credits directly lower the amount of tax owed. Examples include the Work Opportunity Tax Credit for hiring individuals from targeted groups, the Research and Development Tax Credit for innovative projects, and credits for investing in renewable energy or energy-efficient equipment.

Entrepreneurship also offers unique opportunities for long-term wealth creation. By owning and operating a business, you can invest in assets like equipment, vehicles, or real estate, which not only support your operations but also build equity. Depreciation allows you to deduct the cost of these assets over time, further reducing your taxable income while increasing your net worth.

Starting a business isn't just about building something of your own—it's about unlocking a set of financial advantages that can propel your success far beyond what's possible as an employee. By understanding and applying these strategies, you can take full control of your financial future, using the tax code as a powerful ally in achieving your goals.

Maximizing Deductions for Entrepreneurs

One of the most powerful tools at an entrepreneur's disposal is the ability to maximize deductions. Unlike employees, business owners can deduct a wide range of expenses directly related to their operations, allowing them to lower taxable income and keep more of their earnings. These deductions are not just financial perks—they're essential strategies for reinvesting in your business and fueling its growth.

Let's start with operational expenses. Everything from office supplies and software subscriptions to marketing campaigns and utilities can typically be written off. If you operate from a rented space, your lease payments are deductible, as are any utility bills for electricity, water, and internet. For those working from home, the home office deduction provides an opportunity to claim a portion of your rent or mortgage, property taxes, and even homeowners' insurance based on the percentage of your home dedicated to business use.

Travel is another significant deduction for entrepreneurs. Whether it's airfare, hotel stays, or meals during business trips, these expenses are often fully or partially deductible. However, it's important to differentiate between business and personal travel. For example, combining a vacation with a conference trip is permissible, but only the business-related portion of the trip can be deducted. Keeping detailed records, including receipts and itineraries, ensures compliance and maximizes this benefit.

Vehicle expenses also provide entrepreneurs with valuable tax-saving opportunities. If you use a personal vehicle for business purposes, you can deduct either the standard mileage rate or actual expenses, such as fuel, maintenance, and insurance. The standard mileage rate is simpler to track and often preferred, but calculating actual expenses can yield greater savings in some cases, particularly if your vehicle is primarily used for business.

Don't overlook employee-related deductions. Salaries, wages, and benefits provided to employees are fully deductible, making it advantageous to invest in a talented team. Additionally, employer contributions to retirement plans and health insurance are not only deductible but can also serve as recruitment and retention tools.

Continuing education and professional development are essential for staying competitive, and the associated costs are deductible as well. Whether it's attending industry conferences, taking online courses, or purchasing books and training materials, these expenses can reduce your taxable income while enhancing your skills.

Structuring Your Business for Tax Efficiency

The way you structure your business has profound implications for how your income is taxed. Choosing the right entity type isn't just a matter of legal compliance—it's a strategic decision that can save thousands of dollars annually.

Sole proprietorships are the simplest structure, but they offer limited tax advantages. As a sole proprietor, your business income is reported on your personal tax return, and you'll be responsible for self-employment taxes on your earnings. While this structure is easy to set up, it may not provide the flexibility or protection that other options offer.

Limited Liability Companies (LLCs) are a popular choice for small businesses because they combine simplicity with flexibility. LLCs allow profits to pass through to the owner's personal tax return, avoiding double taxation, while offering the option to elect corporate taxation if advantageous. For example, an LLC owner can choose to be taxed as an S corporation to reduce self-employment taxes on distributions, potentially saving a significant amount.

S corporations are particularly beneficial for businesses generating consistent profits. By designating a reasonable salary for the owner and taking the remaining income as distributions, S corporations minimize self-employment taxes while still allowing for deductible employee benefits. This structure is especially advantageous for entrepreneurs in professional services or consulting roles.

For larger businesses or those planning to reinvest heavily, C corporations provide unique benefits. While they are subject to double taxation (at the corporate level and on shareholder dividends), C corporations offer greater flexibility in deducting fringe benefits and reinvesting profits without immediately triggering tax liabilities. Additionally, under Section 1202 of the tax code, gains from the sale of Qualified Small Business Stock (QSBS) in a C corporation can be excluded from capital gains taxes, making this structure appealing for high-growth ventures.

Consider the case of Maria, a graphic designer who transitioned from freelancing to running her own design studio. Initially set up as a sole proprietor, Maria found that her tax burden increased significantly as her income grew. By forming an LLC taxed as an S corporation, she reduced her self-employment taxes and used the savings to hire an assistant. She also invested in a Solo 401(k), sheltering a significant portion of her income from taxes while building a retirement fund. These changes not only improved her cash flow but also set her business on a path for sustainable growth.

Choosing the right structure requires careful analysis of your income, industry, and long-term goals. Consulting with a tax professional is invaluable in making this decision, ensuring that your business is optimized for tax efficiency from the start. By structuring your business strategically, you can take full advantage of the tax code's incentives, setting the stage for long-term success and financial independence.

Chapter 7: International Tax Strategies

The world is more interconnected than ever before, and with that connection comes a wealth of opportunities to optimize your finances on a global scale. International tax strategies are no longer the domain of large corporations and high-net-worth individuals—they're tools accessible to anyone willing to explore the possibilities. Whether you're an entrepreneur expanding into new markets, a remote worker living abroad, or an investor seeking global diversification, understanding international tax strategies can unlock significant savings and provide unparalleled flexibility in managing your wealth.

One of the most impactful benefits of international tax planning is the ability to take advantage of tax treaties between countries. These agreements are designed to prevent double taxation, ensuring that you don't pay taxes on the same income in two jurisdictions. For example, the United States has tax treaties with many countries, allowing U.S. citizens working abroad to exclude a portion of their foreign-earned income from U.S. taxes through the Foreign Earned Income Exclusion

(FEIE). This provision alone can save thousands of dollars each year for individuals working or living overseas.

Relocation to a tax-friendly jurisdiction is another powerful strategy. Countries like the United Arab Emirates, Monaco, and Panama offer low or no income tax, creating opportunities for individuals to drastically reduce their tax burdens. However, this strategy requires careful consideration of residency rules and the potential tax implications in your home country. For instance, U.S. citizens are taxed on their worldwide income regardless of residency, making expatriation a more complex but sometimes necessary step for full tax optimization.

Setting up an offshore business can also yield substantial benefits. By incorporating in countries with favorable tax laws, such as Singapore or Ireland, entrepreneurs can reduce corporate tax rates and streamline international operations. These jurisdictions often provide additional incentives, such as reduced taxes on profits derived from intellectual property or export activities. For small business owners and digital entrepreneurs, this can translate into significant savings that can be reinvested into growth.

Global investment diversification is another key element of international tax strategies. Investing in foreign stocks, bonds, or real estate can not only enhance returns but also provide tax advantages depending on the structure of your portfolio. For instance, many countries offer tax breaks on dividends or capital gains for foreign investors, allowing you to optimize your returns while spreading risk across multiple markets. Additionally, holding investments in tax-advantaged accounts like offshore retirement funds can create opportunities for tax-deferred or tax-free growth.

While the benefits of international tax strategies are clear, navigating the complexities requires diligence and planning. Compliance with both domestic and foreign tax laws is critical to avoid penalties and ensure that your strategies are legally sound. Working with tax professionals who specialize in international law can provide invaluable guidance, helping you identify opportunities while avoiding common pitfalls.

The beauty of international tax strategies lies in their ability to provide flexibility and freedom. They're not just about saving money—they're about creating opportunities to live and work where you choose, grow your wealth in diverse ways, and build a financial plan that aligns with your goals. As you explore these strategies, you'll discover that the world isn't just a marketplace—it's a landscape of possibilities waiting to be unlocked. By taking advantage of what the global tax system has to offer, you're not just managing your wealth—you're designing a life that's as boundless as the opportunities before you.

Exploring Tax-Free Jurisdictions

The allure of tax-free jurisdictions lies in their promise of financial freedom—a way to legally retain more of your hard-earned money while benefiting from streamlined regulations. These jurisdictions, often referred to as tax havens, provide an environment where individuals and businesses can operate with minimal or zero tax liability on income, capital gains, and even inheritances. However, leveraging these opportunities requires a solid understanding of their rules and ethical considerations to ensure compliance with international laws.

Tax-free jurisdictions like the Cayman Islands, Monaco, and the United Arab Emirates (UAE) offer significant advantages for individuals and corporations alike. In many of these locations, income tax simply doesn't exist, making them attractive for high-income earners, digital entrepreneurs, and retirees. For example, the UAE provides a zero-tax environment for most income types, while also offering a robust business infrastructure and high-quality living standards. These benefits, however, come with conditions. To qualify for tax-free treatment, individuals often need to establish legal residency or domicile and meet specific requirements, such as maintaining a minimum number of days in the jurisdiction each year.

For businesses, tax-free jurisdictions like Bermuda or the British Virgin Islands offer corporate structures that minimize tax burdens on international operations. Companies can establish subsidiaries or headquarters in these locations to benefit from low corporate tax rates or exemptions. This is particularly advantageous for industries such as e-commerce, consulting, and intellectual property-based businesses, where physical operations are less critical.

It's crucial to recognize that utilizing tax-free jurisdictions doesn't eliminate all tax obligations. Countries like the United States tax their citizens on worldwide income regardless of where they reside, which means expatriates must carefully navigate reporting requirements.

To avoid penalties, individuals and businesses should adhere to treaties and regulations such as the Foreign Account Tax Compliance Act (FATCA), which mandates reporting foreign assets. Ethical and legal considerations are paramount when exploring these opportunities. Setting up an offshore account or entity without proper documentation or intent can lead to severe penalties, reputational damage, and even criminal charges. Working with qualified legal and tax professionals is essential to ensure compliance and to structure your financial affairs transparently.

Living and Working Abroad Tax-Efficiently

For expatriates and digital nomads, living and working abroad presents a unique opportunity to optimize taxes while embracing a global lifestyle. By strategically planning residency and leveraging tax treaties, it's possible to significantly reduce or even eliminate tax liabilities in certain situations.

One of the most effective tools for expatriates is the Foreign Earned Income Exclusion (FEIE). This U.S. tax provision allows qualifying individuals to exclude a significant portion of their foreign-earned income from taxation—up to $120,000 annually as of recent updates. To qualify, you must meet specific criteria, such as the physical presence test (spending at least 330 days in a foreign country) or establishing bona fide residency in another nation. For digital nomads, carefully planning travel schedules can ensure compliance while maximizing this exclusion.

Tax treaties between countries also play a vital role in minimizing double taxation. Many nations have agreements that specify how income is taxed when earned across borders, ensuring that you don't pay taxes twice on the same income. For example, a treaty between the U.S. and France allows American citizens living in France to avoid double taxation on retirement income and social security benefits. Understanding the provisions of these treaties and how they apply to your situation can unlock substantial savings.

Residency rules are another critical factor in managing taxes abroad. Some countries, like Portugal, offer special tax regimes for new residents. The Portuguese Non-Habitual Resident (NHR) program, for instance, provides a 10-year period of reduced or zero taxation on certain types of foreign income. Similarly, Thailand's Smart Visa and Malaysia's My Second Home program cater to digital nomads and retirees, offering long-term visas and favorable tax treatment.

Navigating the complexities of international tax laws may seem daunting, but breaking them down into actionable steps simplifies the process. First, research the residency and tax rules of your destination country. Determine how long you can stay before triggering tax obligations and whether you qualify for special incentives. Next, maintain meticulous records of your income, expenses, and travel to ensure compliance with both local and home-country regulations. Finally, work with a tax advisor who specializes in international law to identify opportunities and avoid pitfalls.

Living and working abroad isn't just a lifestyle choice—it's a financial strategy. By embracing the flexibility of remote work and understanding the tax benefits available, you can create a sustainable, tax-efficient plan that aligns with your personal and professional goals. The key lies in preparation and a willingness to adapt to the unique requirements of each country, turning global mobility into a powerful tool for wealth preservation.

Offshore Accounts: What's Legal and What's Not

Offshore accounts often evoke images of secrecy, exotic islands, and shadowy financial dealings. However, the reality is far more nuanced—and legal. Opening an offshore account can be a powerful financial tool, offering benefits such as asset protection, currency diversification, and access to tax-efficient strategies. The key lies in understanding what's permissible under the law and ensuring full compliance with both domestic and international regulations. Far from being the domain of the ultra-wealthy, offshore accounts are accessible to everyday individuals and businesses looking to manage their wealth effectively in a globalized world.

Legally opening and maintaining an offshore account starts with choosing the right jurisdiction. Countries like Switzerland, Singapore, and the Cayman Islands are renowned for their stable financial systems, strict privacy laws, and investor-friendly environments. However, opening an account in these jurisdictions does not mean you can avoid your home country's tax obligations.

Transparency is crucial, and many countries now participate in global information-sharing agreements, such as the Common Reporting Standard (CRS) and the Foreign Account Tax Compliance Act (FATCA). These initiatives ensure that governments can track foreign-held assets and income, making it nearly impossible to hide funds offshore without detection.

The benefits of offshore accounts are numerous. They provide access to a wide range of investment opportunities unavailable in some domestic markets, including foreign equities, bonds, and real estate. For expatriates or digital nomads earning income in multiple currencies, offshore accounts can simplify financial management by offering multi-currency banking and reducing the costs associated with currency conversion. Additionally, offshore accounts are often used for asset protection. By holding funds in a politically and economically stable jurisdiction, account holders can shield their wealth from risks such as lawsuits, political instability, or unfavorable domestic financial policies.

However, the legality of offshore accounts hinges on proper reporting. In the United States, for example, citizens and residents must disclose foreign financial accounts exceeding $10,000 in aggregate value through the Foreign Bank Account Report (FBAR) and may also need to file Form 8938 for foreign assets. Failure to comply with these requirements can result in severe penalties, including hefty fines and, in extreme cases, criminal charges. Similar reporting rules exist in many other countries, making it essential to stay informed about your home country's regulations.

Ethical considerations are equally important when using offshore accounts. While these accounts are legal, using them to evade taxes crosses the line into illegal territory. Tax evasion involves deliberately concealing income or assets to avoid taxation and carries significant legal consequences. Tax avoidance, on the other hand, involves using legal strategies to minimize tax liabilities and is entirely permissible. The distinction is critical, and working with experienced professionals can help ensure that your offshore strategies remain above board.

For those interested in opening an offshore account, the process involves several steps. First, research jurisdictions that align with your financial goals, whether that's tax efficiency, investment opportunities, or asset protection. Next, gather the necessary documentation, such as proof of identity, proof of address, and information about the source of funds. Many jurisdictions require thorough due diligence to comply with anti-money laundering laws, so transparency is essential. Finally, consult with a financial advisor or tax professional who specializes in international law to guide you through the process and ensure compliance with all reporting requirements.

A well-structured offshore account can be a valuable addition to your financial toolkit. It offers flexibility, security, and access to global opportunities that can enhance your wealth management strategy. However, the power of offshore accounts lies not in secrecy but in their strategic use within the bounds of the law. By embracing transparency and ethical practices, you can leverage these accounts to achieve your financial goals while maintaining peace of mind. In a world where financial boundaries are increasingly fluid, offshore accounts provide a bridge to greater financial freedom and resilience.

Chapter 8: Retirement Planning Without the Tax Burden

Retirement is often seen as the reward for decades of hard work, but for many, it comes with an unwelcome reality: taxes. Even after years of careful saving, a substantial portion of your retirement income could be siphoned off by the tax system unless you plan wisely. However, with the right strategies, it's possible to build a retirement plan that minimizes taxes and maximizes your hard-earned wealth, allowing you to fully enjoy the fruits of your labor.

The foundation of a tax-free retirement lies in choosing the right investment vehicles. Roth IRAs and Roth 401(k)s stand out as some of the most powerful tools available. Unlike traditional accounts that offer a tax deduction upfront, Roth accounts are funded with after-tax dollars. This means that when you withdraw funds during retirement, they come out completely tax-free—both the contributions and the growth. For someone starting early, this can mean hundreds of thousands of dollars of untaxed income in retirement. The longer your contributions have to grow, the greater the benefit, making Roth accounts a cornerstone of any tax-efficient retirement strategy.

Health Savings Accounts (HSAs) are another underutilized yet incredibly effective tool for retirement planning. These accounts offer a rare triple tax advantage: contributions are tax-deductible, earnings grow tax-free, and withdrawals for qualified medical expenses are untaxed. Given that healthcare costs are one of the largest expenses in retirement, an HSA can serve as both a short-term tax break and a long-term safety net. After age 65, withdrawals for non-medical expenses are taxed at ordinary income rates, similar to a traditional IRA, but strategic use of this account for healthcare spending can keep it entirely tax-free.

Beyond specific accounts, the way you structure your withdrawals in retirement can have a profound impact on your tax burden. Most retirees draw from their taxable accounts, traditional IRAs, and Roth accounts in that order, but this isn't always the most efficient approach. For example, withdrawing from a mix of accounts can help you stay within lower tax brackets, reducing the overall taxes you pay. Carefully coordinating Social

Security benefits with withdrawals can also minimize taxes, as up to 85% of Social Security income can be taxed if your other income exceeds certain thresholds.

Real estate can play a significant role in tax-free retirement planning as well. By downsizing or relocating to a tax-friendly state, retirees can reduce property taxes and other living expenses. Additionally, the sale of a primary residence often allows for capital gains exclusions of up to $250,000 for individuals and $500,000 for married couples, providing a tax-free infusion of cash that can be reinvested or used to fund retirement goals.

Another often-overlooked strategy involves gifting and charitable contributions. For retirees with significant wealth, making annual gifts to family members or donating to qualified charities can reduce the taxable portion of an estate, ensuring that more of their money goes to loved ones or causes they care about rather than to taxes. Qualified Charitable Distributions (QCDs) from traditional IRAs are particularly useful for those over 70½, allowing them to satisfy required minimum distributions (RMDs) while keeping the withdrawn amount excluded from taxable income.

Planning a tax-free retirement is not just about saving more—it's about saving smarter. By understanding the tax implications of different accounts, structuring withdrawals strategically, and leveraging tools like real estate and charitable giving, you can build a plan that protects your wealth and provides financial freedom. Retirement should be a time of relaxation and enjoyment, not stress over taxes. With the right strategies in place, you can ensure that the money you've worked so hard to save stays in your pocket, funding the lifestyle you've always envisioned.

Building a Tax-Free Retirement Portfolio

Creating a retirement portfolio that minimizes taxes is not just about saving diligently—it's about saving strategically. The tax code offers numerous tools to help you grow your wealth without unnecessary tax erosion, but building a truly tax-free retirement portfolio requires careful planning, informed decision-making, and a clear understanding of how different investment vehicles work together. By leveraging accounts like Roth IRAs, Health Savings Accounts (HSAs), and tax-advantaged annuities, you can design a retirement strategy that preserves more of your hard-earned money while providing financial freedom in your golden years.

A cornerstone of any tax-free retirement portfolio is the Roth IRA. This account stands out for its ability to grow investments tax-free, offering withdrawals in retirement that are completely untaxed. Unlike traditional IRAs, Roth IRAs require contributions with after-tax dollars, meaning you don't get an upfront tax deduction. However, the trade-off is well worth it. By paying taxes now, you lock in tax-free growth for life, shielding both your contributions and investment earnings from future taxation. For individuals just starting their careers or expecting to be in higher tax brackets later in life, Roth IRAs are especially advantageous.

Roth 401(k)s offer similar benefits for those with access to employer-sponsored plans. These accounts combine the tax-free growth of a Roth IRA with the higher contribution limits of a traditional 401(k), allowing you to save more aggressively. Some employers also offer matching contributions, further amplifying the value of this tool. By maximizing contributions to both Roth IRAs and Roth 401(k)s, you create a solid foundation for tax-free income in retirement.

Health Savings Accounts (HSAs) add another layer of tax efficiency. While they're often overlooked as a retirement planning tool, HSAs offer a unique triple tax advantage. Contributions are tax-deductible, earnings grow tax-free, and withdrawals for qualified medical expenses are untaxed. Given that healthcare costs are one of the largest expenses retirees face, an HSA can be a powerful resource. By funding this account early and allowing it to grow, you can build a significant reserve for medical expenses while keeping your retirement income untouched by taxes.

Tax-advantaged annuities are another option for those seeking a steady income stream without the tax burden. These products allow your investments to grow tax-deferred until you start receiving payments. While withdrawals are typically taxed at ordinary income rates, pairing annuities with other tax-efficient strategies—such as Roth conversions or blending withdrawals from different account types—can reduce overall tax liability. Additionally, some annuities offer riders that provide guaranteed income, ensuring stability while optimizing tax outcomes.

One of the most common mistakes people make in retirement planning is failing to diversify their tax exposure. Many retirees rely too heavily on tax-deferred accounts like traditional IRAs and 401(k)s, only to face steep tax bills when required minimum distributions (RMDs) begin. A well-structured portfolio balances tax-deferred, tax-free, and taxable accounts, providing flexibility and reducing the likelihood of being pushed into higher tax brackets.

Withdrawal strategies also play a crucial role in minimizing taxes. The traditional approach of drawing first from taxable accounts, then tax-deferred accounts, and finally tax-free accounts isn't always optimal. For example, blending withdrawals from Roth IRAs and tax-deferred accounts can help you stay within lower tax brackets while preserving the longevity of your savings. Timing Social Security benefits strategically can further reduce taxes, as up to 85% of Social Security income may be taxable if other income exceeds certain thresholds.

To avoid costly mistakes, it's essential to start planning early and revisit your strategy regularly. Life events, market conditions, and changes in tax laws can all impact your retirement plan. Working with a financial advisor who specializes in tax-efficient strategies ensures that your portfolio adapts to these changes while staying aligned with your goals.

Building a tax-free retirement portfolio isn't about taking shortcuts—it's about making smart, intentional choices. By combining the right investment vehicles with thoughtful withdrawal strategies, you can maximize your income, protect your wealth, and enjoy the peace of mind that comes with a financially secure retirement. Retirement is your reward for years of hard work, and with the right approach, it can also be a time of unparalleled financial freedom.

The Role of Roth Accounts and Annuities

When it comes to planning a tax-efficient retirement, Roth accounts and annuities stand out as indispensable tools. Together, they create a robust foundation for generating income while minimizing tax liabilities, ensuring that retirees can focus on enjoying their golden years without the stress of unexpected tax bills. Both options offer unique advantages, and understanding how to integrate them into your retirement strategy can lead to long-term financial security.

Roth accounts, including Roth IRAs and Roth 401(k)s, are the crown jewels of tax-free retirement planning. Unlike traditional accounts that defer taxes until withdrawal, Roth accounts require you to pay taxes on contributions upfront. This strategic trade-off allows your investments to grow completely tax-free, and when it's time to access the funds, withdrawals—both contributions and earnings—are untaxed. This can be a game-changer in retirement, especially for individuals who anticipate being in higher tax brackets or who want to avoid the impact of required minimum distributions (RMDs).

Take the example of a couple in their 30s contributing $6,500 annually to their Roth IRAs. Over 30 years, with an average annual return of 7%, their accounts could grow to nearly $1 million. By choosing Roth accounts, they've created a tax-free reservoir of wealth that can be accessed without worrying about tax brackets or penalties. This freedom not only enhances financial stability but also provides flexibility in managing other income sources, such as Social Security or taxable accounts.

Annuities complement Roth accounts by offering predictable income streams with tax-deferred growth. While Roth accounts are excellent for long-term tax-free growth, annuities shine when retirees seek guaranteed income for life. Fixed annuities provide steady payments, while variable annuities allow investment growth tied to market performance. Both options offer tax-deferred growth, meaning you don't pay taxes on earnings until you start receiving payments.

A tax-advantaged annuity can be particularly valuable for retirees who want to lock in income without depleting their principal investments. For instance, someone with $500,000 in a tax-deferred annuity could use it to generate consistent monthly income while allowing other investments to grow untouched. Additionally, pairing an annuity with a Roth conversion strategy can further minimize taxes, as withdrawals from the annuity can be offset by the tax-free nature of the Roth account.

The key to leveraging Roth accounts and annuities effectively is balance. Roth accounts offer flexibility and tax-free growth, while annuities provide stability and predictability. Together, they create a comprehensive retirement strategy that reduces tax burdens and enhances peace of mind.

Minimizing Taxes in Retirement Withdrawals

Withdrawal strategies are one of the most overlooked yet critical components of tax-efficient retirement planning. How you access your savings in retirement can dramatically affect how much you pay in taxes, how long your funds last, and even your eligibility for certain benefits. By carefully structuring withdrawals, retirees can maximize income while keeping taxes to a minimum.

One common mistake is withdrawing too much from tax-deferred accounts like traditional IRAs and 401(k)s early in retirement. These withdrawals are taxed as ordinary income and can push retirees into higher tax brackets, significantly increasing their tax bills. To avoid this, retirees should consider blending withdrawals from multiple account types. For example, withdrawing some income from taxable accounts, Roth accounts, and tax-deferred accounts in a coordinated way can help spread out tax liabilities and keep overall taxes low.

Roth accounts play a critical role in this strategy. Since Roth withdrawals are tax-free, they can be used to supplement income without affecting your tax bracket. This is especially valuable when other income sources, such as Social Security or annuities, push you close to a higher bracket. For instance, if you're approaching the threshold where up to 85% of your Social Security benefits become taxable, using Roth funds can help you stay below that limit.

Taxable accounts are another important piece of the puzzle. Long-term capital gains and qualified dividends are often taxed at lower rates than ordinary income, making them an efficient source of income in retirement. However, retirees should be mindful of how capital gains interact with other income. Selling appreciated assets strategically, such as in years with lower income, can help reduce or eliminate taxes on gains.

The timing of required minimum distributions (RMDs) is another factor to consider. Starting at age 73 (or 72, depending on your birth year), retirees must begin withdrawing a minimum amount from traditional IRAs and 401(k)s. These distributions are fully taxable and can cause a significant tax spike if not planned for. One effective strategy to mitigate this is to use Roth conversions in the years leading up to RMDs. By converting portions of a traditional IRA to a Roth IRA while still in a lower tax bracket, you reduce the balance subject to future RMDs and create additional tax-free income.

Another strategy involves using Qualified Charitable Distributions (QCDs) to minimize taxes on RMDs. Retirees over 70½ can donate up to $100,000 per year directly from their IRA to a qualified charity, satisfying their RMD requirement while keeping the withdrawal excluded from taxable income. This approach not only reduces taxes but also supports causes retirees care about.

Crafting a withdrawal strategy requires ongoing attention and adaptation. Tax laws, investment performance, and personal circumstances can all change over time, making flexibility essential. By working with a financial advisor and staying informed, retirees can navigate these complexities and ensure that their wealth lasts as long as they do—while minimizing what goes to the taxman.

Chapter 9: Tax-Free Living for Families

Raising a family is one of life's greatest joys, but it also comes with its share of financial challenges. Balancing education, healthcare, housing, and everyday living expenses often feels like a juggling act. Yet, within the complexities of family finances lies an opportunity: the ability to leverage the tax system to your advantage. By understanding the tax benefits available to families, you can free up resources, build a more secure financial foundation, and create a lifestyle that aligns with your goals without the constant pressure of overwhelming expenses.

Families have unique needs, and fortunately, the tax code offers specific provisions designed to alleviate the financial burdens of raising children and supporting dependents. One of the most powerful tools is the Child Tax Credit. This credit provides a direct reduction of your tax bill for each qualifying child, making it significantly more impactful than deductions that only reduce taxable income. Depending on your income level, this credit can put thousands of dollars back in your pocket each year, allowing you to reinvest in your family's future or cover essential expenses.

For families with childcare expenses, the Child and Dependent Care Credit offers additional relief. Whether you're paying for daycare, after-school programs, or a babysitter, a portion of these costs can be claimed as a credit on your tax return. This benefit is particularly valuable for working parents who rely on childcare to maintain their careers while ensuring their children are cared for in a safe and nurturing environment.

Education is another significant expense for families, but tax-advantaged accounts like 529 plans make it easier to save for college without the burden of taxes. Contributions to these plans grow tax-free, and withdrawals are untaxed as long as they're used for qualified educational expenses such as tuition, books, or room and board. Some states even offer additional tax benefits for contributions, providing families with a double advantage. For those with younger children, Coverdell Education Savings Accounts (ESAs) can also be used to fund private K-12 schooling, offering flexibility in educational planning.

Healthcare costs can be a major concern for families, but tools like Health Savings Accounts (HSAs) provide a way to save tax-free for medical expenses. HSAs allow families with high-deductible health plans to contribute pre-tax dollars, which grow tax-free and can be withdrawn tax-free for qualified expenses. This triple tax benefit makes HSAs an essential part of a family's financial toolkit, especially as healthcare expenses continue to rise.

Housing is another area where families can find tax relief. The mortgage interest deduction is a cornerstone benefit for homeowners, reducing taxable income by allowing you to deduct interest paid on a home loan. Families who sell their primary residence can also take advantage of the capital gains exclusion, which allows you to exclude up to $500,000 of profit from taxes if you meet residency requirements. This benefit can be a game-changer for families looking to upgrade to a larger home or relocate for better opportunities.

One often-overlooked strategy for families is income shifting. By hiring your children to work in your family business or perform age-appropriate tasks, you can shift income to a lower tax bracket.

Not only does this reduce your overall tax burden, but it also teaches your children valuable financial skills and work ethics. This strategy, when done correctly, is perfectly legal and provides both immediate and long-term benefits for the entire family.

The key to tax-free living for families is proactive planning and awareness of the opportunities available. By leveraging tax credits, deductions, and savings accounts tailored to family needs, you can optimize your finances while focusing on what truly matters: creating meaningful experiences and a secure future for your loved ones. Raising a family may come with financial pressures, but with the right strategies, those pressures can transform into possibilities, opening doors to a more prosperous and fulfilling family life.

Education Savings Plans and Tax Benefits

Education is one of the most significant investments a family can make, and the rising costs of tuition, books, and other related expenses can feel overwhelming. Fortunately, education savings plans like 529 accounts and Coverdell Education Savings Accounts (ESAs) offer families a way to plan for these expenses while taking advantage of powerful tax benefits. Understanding how to use these accounts effectively can make the difference between a manageable education fund and financial strain.

The 529 plan is one of the most popular tools for education savings due to its flexibility and tax advantages. Contributions to a 529 plan grow tax-free, and withdrawals are untaxed as long as they're used for qualified education expenses. These include tuition, books, and even room and board for college students. In recent years, 529 plans have been expanded to cover K-12 private school tuition, making them a valuable tool for families planning private or alternative education. Some states even offer tax deductions or credits for contributions to a 529 plan, providing an additional incentive for parents to start saving early.

Take the example of James and Maria, who began contributing $200 a month to a 529 plan when their daughter Sophia was born. By the time Sophia turned 18, their consistent contributions, coupled with compounding growth, resulted in a fund of nearly $70,000. Because they used a tax-advantaged plan, every dollar of growth in the account went toward Sophia's tuition, rather than being reduced by taxes. This proactive planning allowed them to focus on Sophia's education rather than scrambling to find financial resources when she started college.

Coverdell ESAs are another option, offering similar tax-free growth and withdrawal benefits. While they have lower contribution limits than 529 plans, they provide greater investment flexibility and can be used for K-12 expenses as well as higher education. For families with diverse education needs, combining a 529 plan and a Coverdell ESA can provide the best of both worlds, allowing parents to optimize their savings strategies while reaping significant tax benefits.

Beyond savings accounts, parents should explore education tax credits such as the American Opportunity Tax Credit (AOTC) and the Lifetime Learning Credit (LLC). The AOTC provides up to $2,500 per eligible student for tuition and related expenses, while the LLC offers up to $2,000 per tax return for continuing education. These credits can be combined with education savings plans for maximum tax efficiency, allowing families to stretch their dollars even further.

Estate Planning and Inheritance Tax Strategies

Passing on wealth to the next generation is a priority for many families, but without careful planning, a significant portion of that wealth can be lost to taxes. Estate planning is essential for preserving assets, minimizing taxes, and ensuring that your financial legacy benefits your loved ones.

One of the most effective tools in estate planning is the annual gift tax exclusion. This allows individuals to gift up to a certain amount—currently $16,000 per recipient per year—without triggering gift taxes or impacting their lifetime estate tax exemption. For example, a couple with three children could collectively gift $96,000 each year to their children and grandchildren, gradually transferring wealth tax-free while reducing the size of their taxable estate.

Trusts are another cornerstone of estate planning, offering both flexibility and tax benefits. A revocable living trust allows families to manage their assets during their lifetime while avoiding the lengthy and costly probate process after death. For those with significant assets, irrevocable trusts can be used to remove assets from the taxable estate entirely, providing protection from estate taxes while ensuring that the assets are distributed according to the family's wishes.

Consider the scenario of Alan and Lisa, a couple with a net worth of $5 million. By setting up an irrevocable life insurance trust (ILIT), they transferred their life insurance policy out of their estate, ensuring that the proceeds would pass to their children without being subject to estate taxes. This single step saved their family hundreds of thousands of dollars in taxes, preserving their financial legacy.

Families should also explore state-specific estate tax laws, as some states impose estate taxes in addition to federal taxes. Relocating to a state without an estate tax or implementing tax-efficient strategies tailored to local laws can provide significant savings.

Charitable giving is another powerful estate planning strategy. Donations to qualified charities not only reduce the size of the taxable estate but also align with the family's values and philanthropic goals. Qualified Charitable Distributions (QCDs) from traditional IRAs are particularly effective, allowing retirees over age 70½ to satisfy their required minimum distributions (RMDs) while excluding the withdrawal from taxable income.

By combining these strategies, families can reduce the impact of estate and inheritance taxes while ensuring that their wealth benefits the people and causes they care about most. Estate planning is not just about minimizing taxes—it's about creating a legacy that reflects your priorities and secures your family's future. Starting the process early and working with experienced professionals ensures that your financial legacy is as impactful as it is protected.

Passing on Wealth Tax-Free

For many families, leaving a financial legacy is about more than just transferring assets; it's about ensuring that their loved ones are set up for success without the burden of taxes reducing the value of what's passed on. Fortunately, with the right strategies, families can transfer wealth tax-free or with minimal tax liabilities. Estate planning isn't just for the ultra-wealthy—it's an essential process for any family seeking to protect and preserve what they've built over generations.

One of the simplest and most effective tools for passing on wealth tax-free is the annual gift tax exclusion. This provision allows individuals to give up to $16,000 per year per recipient without triggering gift taxes or affecting their lifetime estate tax exemption. Married couples can double this amount, gifting up to $32,000 per recipient annually. Over time, these gifts can add up to substantial tax-free wealth transfers. For instance, a couple with three children and five grandchildren could gift $320,000 each year collectively, reducing their taxable estate while ensuring that their family benefits from their generosity in real-time.

Trusts are another cornerstone of tax-free wealth transfer. Irrevocable trusts, in particular, are powerful tools for removing assets from the taxable estate while retaining control over how and when beneficiaries receive the funds. A popular option is the irrevocable life insurance trust (ILIT), which allows the proceeds of a life insurance policy to be excluded from the taxable estate. For example, a family can place a $1 million life insurance policy into an ILIT, ensuring that the full amount passes to their heirs without being reduced by estate taxes. This strategy is especially effective for families with significant life insurance policies or those looking to create liquidity for their heirs.

Grantor Retained Annuity Trusts (GRATs) are also worth considering for families with appreciating assets. With a GRAT, the grantor transfers assets into the trust while retaining the right to receive an annuity payment for a set number of years. At the end of the term, any remaining value in the trust passes to the beneficiaries tax-free. This strategy works best for assets expected to grow significantly in value, such as stocks, real estate, or business interests.

For families with philanthropic goals, charitable giving is a dual-purpose strategy that reduces taxes while supporting meaningful causes. Donations to qualified charities not only provide immediate income tax deductions but also reduce the size of the taxable estate. Donor-advised funds and charitable remainder trusts allow families to give strategically, ensuring that their wealth has a lasting impact. For retirees, Qualified Charitable Distributions (QCDs) from traditional IRAs are a particularly effective way to reduce required minimum distributions (RMDs) and their associated taxes.

Another key aspect of passing on wealth tax-free is choosing the right state for estate and inheritance taxes. While the federal estate tax exemption is currently $12.92 million per individual, some states have their own estate or inheritance taxes with much lower thresholds. Families can benefit from relocating to states without these taxes, such as Florida or Texas, to maximize the amount of wealth that passes to their heirs.

Consider the story of Emily, a grandmother who wanted to ensure her grandchildren's futures were secure. She established 529 plans for each grandchild, contributing $80,000 to each account in a single year under the special five-year election rule, which allows individuals to front-load contributions without incurring gift taxes. This strategy removed $480,000 from her taxable estate while funding her grandchildren's education tax-free. Emily also created an ILIT to shield her $2 million life insurance policy from estate taxes, ensuring that the full benefit would pass to her children. By combining these strategies, Emily created a comprehensive plan that protected her legacy and empowered her family.

The key to successful wealth transfer lies in proactive planning. Waiting too long can lead to missed opportunities, unnecessary taxes, and potential conflicts among heirs. By starting early and working with qualified professionals, families can ensure their wishes are carried out efficiently and that their wealth serves its intended purpose. Passing on wealth is about more than numbers—it's about securing a family's future and creating a lasting impact for generations to come. Families who take the time to plan today can rest assured that they're leaving behind not just assets, but a legacy of thoughtful care and financial stability.

Chapter 10. The Legal Side of Tax-Free Living

Navigating the world of tax-free living is like walking a fine line between opportunity and compliance. On one side, there's a treasure trove of legal strategies to minimize taxes and maximize wealth; on the other, there's the risk of crossing boundaries that could result in penalties, audits, or even legal trouble. The key to thriving within this space lies in understanding the legal framework that governs tax-free strategies, ensuring that every decision you make is backed by both knowledge and integrity. Tax-free living is not about evasion; it's about using the system to your advantage while respecting its rules.

Every tax-saving strategy you employ must start with clarity about the laws that apply to your specific situation. Tax codes, while complex, are designed with incentives that encourage behaviors like saving for retirement, investing in education, and supporting the economy through entrepreneurship. These provisions are not loopholes—they are deliberate opportunities offered by governments to help citizens build wealth while aligning with national priorities.

Knowing how to access these incentives legally is the cornerstone of any tax-free plan.

For example, when leveraging Roth IRAs or Health Savings Accounts, the tax advantages are crystal clear, as long as you follow contribution limits and withdrawal rules. Similarly, taking advantage of tax credits, like the Child Tax Credit or the American Opportunity Tax Credit, requires accurate reporting of income, expenses, and eligibility. One misstep—whether accidental or intentional—can not only negate these benefits but also trigger audits or fines.

The legal side of tax-free living also involves keeping impeccable records. Whether you're claiming deductions for business expenses, documenting charitable contributions, or tracking education-related withdrawals from a 529 plan, maintaining organized and detailed records is non-negotiable. In the event of an audit, these records become your defense, proving that your claims are legitimate and compliant with the law. Tax preparation software and professional advisors can be invaluable in ensuring that every entry is accurate and well-documented.

Another critical aspect is understanding the international dimensions of tax law if your strategy involves offshore accounts, overseas income, or relocation to a tax-friendly country. While jurisdictions like the Cayman Islands or the United Arab Emirates offer enticing tax benefits, compliance with international reporting requirements, such as the Foreign Account Tax Compliance Act (FATCA) or the Common Reporting Standard (CRS), is essential. These frameworks exist to ensure transparency and prevent illegal tax evasion. Navigating them successfully requires a deep understanding of both local and home-country regulations.

One of the most common pitfalls in tax-free planning is confusing avoidance with evasion. Tax avoidance, which involves legally reducing your tax liability, is entirely permissible and encouraged by the tax code. Tax evasion, on the other hand, is the illegal act of concealing income or misrepresenting information to reduce taxes owed. The consequences of evasion are severe, ranging from financial penalties to imprisonment. Staying on the right side of the law means working with qualified tax professionals who can help you identify legitimate strategies and avoid risky or unethical practices.

Consider the case of Rachel, a small business owner who expanded her operations internationally. By working with a tax advisor, she structured her business as an LLC, electing S-corporation status to optimize U.S. tax benefits, while also opening an office in a jurisdiction with favorable tax treaties. Rachel's compliance with reporting requirements and her careful documentation of business expenses ensured that she maximized her savings without jeopardizing her legal standing. Her story highlights how knowledge and proper guidance can transform a complex tax situation into a well-managed, compliant strategy.

The legal framework of tax-free living may seem daunting, but it's also a roadmap to opportunity. By staying informed, working with experienced professionals, and adhering to the rules, you can unlock significant financial benefits while safeguarding your peace of mind. Legal tax-free living is not just about saving money; it's about building a legacy of wealth and security that stands the test of time.

Staying Compliant with Tax Laws

Tax-free living is an exciting prospect, but achieving it requires more than knowing the right strategies—it demands strict compliance with tax laws. The rules are in place not to discourage taxpayers from saving but to ensure fairness and transparency. Staying compliant means not only avoiding legal repercussions but also protecting the financial benefits you've worked so hard to secure. With a solid understanding of the laws, paired with the right resources and professionals, you can confidently navigate the tax system while keeping more of your wealth intact.

The cornerstone of compliance lies in accurate reporting. Whether you're filing as an individual, a small business owner, or an investor, every deduction, credit, and exclusion must be documented and reported accurately. This starts with understanding what qualifies as a legitimate expense or deduction. For instance, if you're deducting home office expenses, you must ensure the space is exclusively used for work. Similarly, when claiming charitable contributions, receipts and documentation of the charity's eligibility are non-negotiable. These records should be organized and stored securely, as they are your best defense in the event of an audit.

A major pitfall for many taxpayers is underestimating the complexity of the tax code. While it's possible to manage your taxes independently, engaging a qualified tax professional often makes the difference between maximizing your benefits and leaving money on the table—or worse, making costly mistakes. Tax professionals bring expertise in identifying opportunities that align with your financial goals while keeping you fully compliant with the law. They can also stay updated on ever-changing tax regulations, ensuring that your strategies evolve as the rules do.

Timing is another critical element of compliance. Filing late or failing to pay estimated taxes can result in penalties and interest that quickly erode your savings. For freelancers and business owners, quarterly estimated tax payments are a common stumbling block. Missing these deadlines not only attracts penalties but can also signal poor financial management, increasing your risk of an audit. Using tools like automated reminders or tax planning software can help ensure that deadlines are never missed.

When it comes to tax-free living, one of the most common legal pitfalls is misunderstanding the difference between tax avoidance and tax evasion. Tax avoidance involves legally reducing your tax liability through methods sanctioned by the tax code, such as contributing to retirement accounts or utilizing tax credits. Tax evasion, on the other hand, is an illegal act of deliberately misrepresenting income, failing to report income, or claiming false deductions. While the line between the two may seem thin, the consequences of stepping over it are severe, ranging from financial penalties to criminal charges.

International compliance is another area where many taxpayers falter, particularly those with offshore accounts or foreign income. Reporting requirements like the Foreign Account Tax Compliance Act (FATCA) and the Foreign Bank Account Report (FBAR) mandate full transparency for U.S. citizens with foreign financial assets. Failure to comply can lead to significant fines and legal action, even for unintentional omissions. For expatriates, digital nomads, or anyone investing abroad, consulting with a tax advisor who specializes in international tax law is essential to staying compliant.

To help you stay on the right side of the law, consider this simple checklist for tax compliance:
- Maintain detailed records of all income, expenses, and deductions, ensuring they align with IRS guidelines.
- Use reliable tax preparation software or hire a qualified professional to file your taxes accurately.
- Stay updated on filing deadlines and make timely payments to avoid penalties.
- Familiarize yourself with specific tax rules that apply to your situation, such as self-employment taxes or foreign income reporting.
- Regularly review your tax strategies with a professional to adapt to any changes in the law.
- Be honest and transparent in all your filings, avoiding any temptations to exaggerate deductions or underreport income.

By following these steps and staying vigilant, you can confidently pursue tax-free living without fear of audits or penalties. Compliance isn't just a legal requirement—it's a safeguard for the financial freedom you're working to achieve. When done right, tax planning becomes a powerful tool, allowing you to take full advantage of the system while maintaining peace of mind. Through diligence and the support of trusted professionals, you can build a tax-free life that's not only rewarding but also legally sound.

Working with Professionals: Accountants and Advisors

The complexities of tax-free living can make navigating the tax code a daunting task, especially when you're dealing with intricate deductions, international accounts, or a mix of business and personal income. This is where the expertise of accountants and financial advisors becomes invaluable. These professionals act as your guides through the maze of tax laws, helping you make informed decisions while ensuring compliance. Knowing when to consult them and what to expect can save you significant time, money, and stress.

Accountants are your go-to experts for preparing accurate tax returns and identifying opportunities to reduce your tax liability. They understand the nuances of tax law, such as eligibility for deductions and credits, and can spot errors or oversights that could trigger audits or penalties. For example, if you're a small business owner claiming a home office deduction, an accountant can help you calculate the exact percentage of your home's expenses that qualify, ensuring your claim is both legal and optimized.

Certified Public Accountants (CPAs) bring additional expertise, often specializing in tax strategies for high-net-worth individuals, businesses, or international clients. They can assist with everything from creating tax-efficient investment portfolios to managing complex inheritance tax scenarios. A CPA's advice can be particularly useful during life events like starting a business, selling property, or relocating abroad, as these situations often come with unique tax implications.

Financial advisors, on the other hand, take a broader approach, focusing on long-term wealth management while incorporating tax efficiency into your financial plan. They can guide you on how to allocate assets in tax-advantaged accounts, such as Roth IRAs or 529 plans, and recommend strategies for minimizing taxes on capital gains.

For individuals nearing retirement, advisors can craft withdrawal plans that balance income needs with tax considerations, ensuring you don't pay more than necessary.

Timing is critical when it comes to involving professionals. Many people wait until the tax filing deadline to seek help, but the real benefits of working with accountants and advisors come from proactive planning. Consulting them at the start of the fiscal year allows you to implement strategies that maximize deductions, credits, and tax-deferred growth opportunities. Annual check-ins also ensure that your financial plan evolves alongside changes in tax law or personal circumstances.

Avoiding Pitfalls and Common Mistakes

While the promise of tax-free living is enticing, the journey isn't without risks. Missteps, whether intentional or accidental, can lead to audits, penalties, or even legal action. Understanding and avoiding these common mistakes is essential for maintaining the integrity of your financial plan and staying on the right side of the law.

One of the most frequent errors is poor record-keeping. Without proper documentation, even legitimate deductions and credits can be disallowed during an audit. For example, if you're claiming business travel expenses, you'll need detailed records of your itinerary, receipts, and the business purpose of each trip. Keeping digital copies of these records, organized by category, ensures that you're prepared if the IRS or your local tax authority comes knocking.

Overestimating or misreporting deductions is another pitfall. While it's tempting to claim the maximum allowable amount, doing so without justification can backfire. This is especially true for deductions like charitable contributions or home office expenses, where exaggerated claims can raise red flags. Using a tax professional or reputable tax software can help you avoid these errors by calculating deductions accurately based on your specific situation.

Failing to stay informed about tax law changes is a common issue that can lead to missed opportunities or inadvertent non-compliance. For instance, updates to retirement contribution limits, tax credit eligibility, or foreign reporting requirements can significantly impact your financial plan. Regularly consulting with professionals or subscribing to trusted tax publications ensures that you stay ahead of the curve.

Another frequent mistake is mixing personal and business finances, particularly among small business owners and freelancers. Without clear separation, it becomes challenging to track deductible expenses, and you risk complications during audits. Setting up dedicated business bank accounts and credit cards simplifies record-keeping and reinforces the legitimacy of your claims.

To help you avoid these pitfalls, consider this checklist:

- Keep meticulous records of income, expenses, and deductions, using digital tools or apps for organization.
- Consult tax professionals at least once a year, especially if your financial situation changes.
- Stay updated on tax law changes that could affect your strategies.

- Use reputable tax preparation software or services to minimize errors.
- Separate personal and business finances with dedicated accounts.
- Double-check all claims for accuracy and ensure you have supporting documentation.

Avoiding mistakes isn't about perfection—it's about being diligent and informed. With the right precautions and professional guidance, you can confidently pursue tax-free living while mitigating risks. Tax planning isn't just a once-a-year activity; it's an ongoing process that evolves with your life and goals. By staying vigilant and proactive, you ensure that your journey toward financial freedom is both rewarding and legally sound.

Chapter 11: Crafting Your Tax-Free Plan

Creating a tax-free plan is like designing a blueprint for your financial future. It's not just about reducing taxes; it's about taking control of your finances and making deliberate choices that align with your life goals. A well-crafted plan offers clarity, flexibility, and peace of mind, ensuring that you're not only compliant with tax laws but also optimizing every opportunity available to you. Whether you're just starting out or revisiting your current strategy, the process of crafting your tax-free plan is an empowering step toward long-term financial freedom.

The first step is understanding your current financial situation. This means taking a close look at your income streams, expenses, savings, and investments. Are you maximizing tax-advantaged accounts like Roth IRAs, HSAs, or 529 plans? Are you tracking and categorizing expenses to identify deductions and credits you might be missing? A clear picture of your financial landscape serves as the foundation for building a strategy that works for you.

Once you've assessed where you stand, it's time to define your goals. Do you want to save for retirement, fund your child's education, or invest in a business? Perhaps you're planning to relocate to a tax-friendly jurisdiction or diversify your income through real estate. Whatever your objectives, they will shape the decisions you make and the tools you use. For example, if retirement savings is your priority, Roth accounts might take center stage in your plan. If education is a focus, 529 plans could be your best ally.

Timing plays a critical role in tax planning. Contributions to accounts, withdrawals, and even charitable giving all have optimal timeframes to maximize their impact. For instance, contributing early to a Roth IRA allows your investments more time to grow tax-free. Similarly, timing charitable donations strategically can reduce taxable income in high-earning years. A well-timed approach ensures that your plan adapts to both your personal milestones and changes in the tax code.

One of the most powerful aspects of a tax-free plan is its ability to integrate multiple strategies. It's not about choosing between retirement accounts, education savings, or real estate—it's about finding ways to combine them effectively. For example, a couple might use their HSA for medical expenses, contribute to a 529 plan for their child's tuition, and invest in a Roth IRA for retirement, all while leveraging tax credits like the Earned Income Tax Credit or the Child Tax Credit. This layered approach creates a robust financial strategy that covers immediate needs and long-term goals.

To ensure your plan remains effective, it's essential to review and adjust it regularly. Tax laws change, life circumstances evolve, and new opportunities arise. A yearly check-in with a tax professional or financial advisor can help you stay on track and adapt your plan as needed. For example, if you receive a windfall or experience a significant life event like marriage, having a flexible plan allows you to make the most of these changes without missing key opportunities.

Crafting a tax-free plan isn't just a financial exercise—it's a declaration of intent. It's about reclaiming control over your money and using it to build the life you want. By taking the time to assess your situation, define your goals, and implement tailored strategies, you set the stage for a future where taxes don't dictate your choices.

Instead, you're empowered to pursue your dreams with confidence, knowing that your plan is working as hard for you as you've worked to create it.

Assessing Your Financial Situation

Before crafting a tax-free plan, you need to know where you stand financially. Think of it as creating a map; without understanding your starting point, it's impossible to chart a clear and effective course toward your goals. Assessing your financial situation is not just about crunching numbers—it's about gaining clarity, identifying strengths and weaknesses, and uncovering opportunities to maximize your wealth while minimizing tax burdens. This process might seem overwhelming, but with the right steps, it can be both manageable and empowering.

Start with the basics: your income and expenses. Take a close look at all your income sources, whether it's a salary, business revenue, rental income, or investment returns. Break these down to understand how each source is taxed and identify areas where you might reduce liabilities.

For instance, if a significant portion of your income comes from self-employment, are you maximizing deductions like home office expenses or equipment depreciation? Similarly, if you have capital gains from investments, are you utilizing tax-loss harvesting to offset them?

Next, scrutinize your expenses. List out all recurring and one-time expenses, categorizing them into necessities, discretionary spending, and business-related costs. This exercise not only helps you track where your money is going but also highlights potential deductions or credits. For example, if you're paying for childcare, are you taking advantage of the Child and Dependent Care Credit? If you're investing in education, are you leveraging tax-advantaged accounts like 529 plans or claiming education-related tax credits?

Assets and liabilities come next. Create a detailed inventory of your assets, including savings accounts, investments, real estate, and retirement accounts. Note their current value, tax implications, and growth potential. On the flip side, list your liabilities, such as mortgages, loans, or credit card debt. Understanding your net worth is crucial for creating a tax-free plan that balances wealth preservation with growth. For instance, if you have substantial equity in your home, you might explore tax-free strategies like a home equity line of credit (HELOC) for funding business ventures or investments.

Once you've mapped out your current financial landscape, it's time to set realistic goals. Start with short-term objectives, such as saving for a specific purchase, building an emergency fund, or paying off high-interest debt. Then, focus on long-term goals like retirement, funding a child's education, or buying property. Be specific with these goals—rather than saying, "I want to save for retirement," aim for something measurable like, "I want to save $1 million in a Roth IRA by age 60." Clear goals not only keep you motivated but also help you determine which tax-free strategies to prioritize.

To stay on track, use tools and templates to simplify the process. Budgeting apps like Mint or YNAB can help you monitor income and expenses, while tax software like TurboTax or H&R Block assists with identifying deductions and credits. If you prefer a more hands-on approach, spreadsheets can be a great way to customize your financial tracking and planning.

Motivation plays a significant role in sticking to a tax-free plan. Remember that this journey is about creating a future where you control your finances, not the other way around. Celebrate small wins, like contributing the maximum to a Roth IRA for the year or successfully claiming a new tax credit. These victories reinforce your progress and remind you of the bigger picture.

Finally, don't hesitate to revisit and adjust your plan as needed. Life changes, and so do tax laws. What works for you today might not be ideal tomorrow, and that's okay. The goal is to remain flexible and proactive, ensuring that your plan evolves alongside your circumstances. Assessing your financial situation is not a one-time task but an ongoing practice that empowers you to make informed decisions and stay aligned with your goals. By taking the time to understand your starting point, you set the stage for a tax-free future that's as intentional as it is rewarding.

Setting Short and Long-Term Goals

The foundation of any successful tax-free plan lies in setting clear and achievable goals. These goals act as the compass guiding your financial decisions and ensuring every step you take brings you closer to the life you envision. Without well-defined objectives, it's easy to get sidetracked or overwhelmed by the complexities of tax planning. The key is to break your vision into manageable short-term and long-term milestones, each building upon the other to create lasting financial freedom.

Short-term goals are the stepping stones of your tax-free journey. These might include setting up a tax-advantaged savings account, paying off high-interest debt, or identifying deductions and credits you can claim immediately. Start by looking at your immediate needs and opportunities. For example, if you haven't yet contributed to a Roth IRA for the year, setting a goal to maximize that contribution can give you a quick win while establishing the habit of saving tax-free. Similarly, if you've been overlooking deductions like the home office expense or childcare credits, making it a priority to capture those savings can have an immediate impact on your finances.

To make short-term goals actionable, use specific metrics and deadlines. Instead of saying, “I want to start saving for retirement,” frame your goal as, “I will contribute $500 monthly to my Roth IRA starting this month.” Specificity creates accountability and helps you measure progress. Tools like budgeting apps or financial planners can also keep you organized and focused.

Long-term goals require a broader vision and a commitment to sustained effort. These might include achieving financial independence, funding your children’s education, or retiring comfortably while minimizing taxes. Start by identifying what “success” looks like to you. Is it retiring early? Owning a debt-free home? Passing on a tax-efficient legacy to your children? Once you’ve defined these goals, work backward to determine the steps needed to achieve them.

For example, if your goal is to retire with $1.5 million in a tax-free Roth IRA, calculate how much you need to contribute annually to reach that target. Factor in the expected rate of return and the time you have until retirement. This clarity transforms a seemingly monumental goal into a series of actionable steps, giving you the confidence to move forward.

Staying motivated is crucial when pursuing long-term goals, as the benefits often feel distant. Celebrate small milestones, like hitting your first $10,000 in a Roth IRA or paying off a chunk of your mortgage. These moments remind you of your progress and keep you energized. Surrounding yourself with supportive resources, such as financial advisors, books, or online communities, can also provide encouragement and fresh insights.

Creating an Actionable Tax-Free Living Strategy

An effective tax-free living strategy doesn't happen by chance—it's the result of careful planning, informed decisions, and consistent action. Once you've assessed your financial situation and set your goals, the next step is crafting a strategy that bridges the gap between where you are and where you want to be. This plan should be actionable, adaptable, and tailored to your unique circumstances.

Start by identifying the tools and resources that align with your goals. For instance, if retirement savings is a priority, consider Roth IRAs or Roth 401(k)s for tax-free growth. If education funding is a focus, explore 529 plans or Coverdell Education Savings Accounts. For medical expenses, Health Savings Accounts (HSAs) provide unparalleled tax advantages. By matching your goals to specific financial tools, you create a roadmap that's both effective and efficient.

Next, break your strategy into actionable steps. For example, if your goal is to maximize your Roth IRA contributions, start by determining how much you can set aside each month and automate those contributions to ensure consistency. If you're aiming to save for your child's education, set a target amount and timeline, then create a monthly savings plan using a 529 plan. These steps should be clear, measurable, and tied to specific timelines to keep you on track.

One of the most important aspects of an actionable strategy is staying flexible. Tax laws change, and life circumstances can shift unexpectedly. Periodically review your plan to ensure it still aligns with your goals and the current financial landscape. For example, if contribution limits for retirement accounts increase, adjust your savings to take advantage of the higher limits. Similarly, if you experience a major life event, such as a new job or the birth of a child, revisit your strategy to account for these changes.

Tracking your progress is essential to maintaining momentum. Use tools like spreadsheets, apps, or financial dashboards to monitor your savings, investments, and tax benefits. Regular check-ins—monthly for short-term goals and annually for long-term objectives—allow you to celebrate wins, identify areas for improvement, and make necessary adjustments.

Motivation is the glue that holds your strategy together. Tax-free living is a marathon, not a sprint, and staying focused requires both discipline and inspiration. Remind yourself of the "why" behind your plan: the freedom to retire early, the ability to fund your child's future without debt, or the peace of mind that comes from financial security. Share your goals with trusted friends or family members who can hold you accountable and celebrate your successes.

By combining well-defined goals with an actionable strategy, you create a powerful framework for achieving tax-free living. This approach transforms financial planning from an intimidating task into a manageable and rewarding journey, empowering you to take control of your future and build the life you've always envisioned.

Chapter 12: The Mindset of Wealth and Freedom

Wealth and freedom are more than just the outcome of careful planning—they're a mindset, a way of thinking that shapes every financial decision you make. If you want to live a life where financial independence isn't just a dream but a reality, it starts with how you view money, investments, and the opportunities that come your way. The mindset of wealth and freedom is about shifting from a scarcity mentality, where you see limitations and obstacles, to an abundance mentality, where you recognize opportunities and the power of strategic action.

Many people struggle with the idea of financial freedom because they view wealth as something that happens to a lucky few, rather than something that can be created through consistent effort, wise decision-making, and a strategic approach. To break free from this mindset, you need to understand that wealth is not just about having more money; it's about how you manage, grow, and use it. It's about taking control of your financial destiny and not letting your circumstances dictate the terms of your life.

The first step in adopting a wealth and freedom mindset is to redefine your relationship with money. For too long, many have been taught to work hard, save a little, and get by. But this mindset rarely leads to true wealth. Instead, think of money as a tool—a resource that works for you, not the other way around. When you start seeing money not as a limitation but as a means to create more freedom, you begin to shift how you think about every dollar. Each financial decision becomes a strategic move toward your ultimate goal: freedom from financial stress, the ability to choose your own path, and the security to enjoy life on your own terms.

Adopting a wealth mindset also means embracing the power of long-term thinking. It's easy to focus on short-term gains and instant gratification, but lasting wealth requires patience and discipline. Wealthy individuals often make sacrifices now for bigger rewards later. This doesn't mean you have to live in deprivation, but it does mean you have to prioritize your future self over fleeting comforts. Whether it's investing in tax-advantaged accounts or cutting unnecessary expenses to funnel more into savings, small decisions today can compound over time to create incredible results in the future.

Another aspect of the wealth mindset is taking calculated risks. This doesn't mean reckless behavior or gambling with your future—it's about understanding that wealth often comes from stepping outside your comfort zone and seizing opportunities that align with your long-term goals. Maybe it's starting a business, investing in real estate, or exploring new investment vehicles like stocks or bonds. But, every decision should be made with a clear understanding of the potential benefits and risks involved. When you take calculated risks with your financial resources, you're building the path to a future where your money works for you, rather than the other way around.

Lastly, the mindset of wealth and freedom requires an unwavering belief in your ability to shape your own financial future. So much of wealth-building is mental—it's about believing that you have control and that, with the right strategies, you can grow your wealth. While financial setbacks and challenges may come your way, maintaining a mindset of resilience and perseverance is key to overcoming them. Instead of seeing obstacles as insurmountable, see them as learning experiences or stepping stones to something greater.

Building wealth isn't just about numbers or strategies; it's about how you think about your money and your future. Once you adopt the mindset of wealth and freedom, you'll begin to see opportunities where others see limitations, and you'll find yourself making decisions that move you closer to the life you've always dreamed of. It's not just about getting rich—it's about creating a life where financial freedom empowers you to live fully and without restriction.

Changing How You Think About Money and Taxes

When it comes to financial independence, one of the most powerful tools at your disposal is your mindset. For many, money and taxes are seen as burdens—something to be avoided or minimized. But in reality, the way you think about money, taxes, and wealth plays a huge role in your ability to create financial freedom. Shifting your mindset isn't just about changing your thoughts; it's about transforming your entire approach to life, money, and opportunity.

To start, consider how you currently view money. Do you see it as a scarce resource that must be tightly controlled and hoarded, or do you view it as a tool for growth and opportunity? Successful individuals understand that wealth is not about saving every penny but about making money work for them. They see money as a resource that can be used to leverage more wealth, whether through investments, businesses, or other income-generating activities. Shifting from a mindset of scarcity to one of abundance is crucial for building tax-free wealth. Instead of focusing solely on how much you can save, think about how you can use what you have to create more wealth in ways that align with your long-term goals.

Equally important is changing the way you think about taxes. Taxes are often seen as an unavoidable expense that drains your hard-earned money, but a shift in perspective reveals a different truth: taxes are a part of a system that rewards strategic planning and investment. Successful individuals don't view taxes as a punishment; they see them as an opportunity to leverage tax-saving strategies that minimize their liability and maximize their wealth. Tax-free wealth is built by understanding the system, identifying available benefits, and using those strategies to your advantage.

One of the most effective ways to cultivate this mindset is by adopting the habits of financially successful individuals. These habits go beyond the traditional "save and budget" advice and focus on how to work smarter with your money. Wealthy individuals tend to prioritize investments that provide long-term, tax-advantaged growth, such as Roth IRAs, 529 education plans, and real estate. They understand the importance of compound interest and are always looking for ways to make their money grow without paying unnecessary taxes along the way.

Another key habit is lifelong learning. Financially successful people consistently educate themselves on topics like tax law, investment strategies, and personal finance. They don't rely solely on traditional methods of saving and investing—they actively seek out knowledge and advice from experts to ensure they are maximizing every opportunity. Whether it's reading books, attending seminars, or hiring financial advisors, these individuals understand that knowledge is power, especially when it comes to money and taxes.

Overcoming fear, procrastination, or misinformation about taxes is another crucial part of this mindset shift. The idea of navigating tax laws or facing an audit can cause a lot of anxiety, and that fear can often lead to avoidance or inaction. However, the more you learn about the system and take proactive steps, the less intimidating it becomes. Understanding the benefits of tax-deferred accounts, tax credits, and deductions can take the fear out of taxes, allowing you to embrace strategies that work in your favor.

Procrastination also plays a significant role in hindering financial progress. Putting off tax planning or delaying savings and investments can cause you to miss out on opportunities that could benefit you in the long run. To combat procrastination, set clear, actionable goals and break them down into smaller, manageable steps. For example, instead of saying, "I need to save more for retirement," focus on the specific actions needed, such as, "I will contribute $500 to my Roth IRA every month." The more focused and actionable your goals, the less likely you are to put them off.

Misinformation about taxes can also create unnecessary obstacles. Many people don't fully understand the tax benefits available to them or mistakenly believe that they're not eligible for certain tax advantages. For example, some might think they make too much money to contribute to a Roth IRA, but there are ways to contribute even if your income exceeds the standard limits, such as through the backdoor Roth IRA strategy. Seeking accurate information, whether through professional advice or reliable resources, will ensure you're making informed decisions that work in your favor.

As you work to shift your mindset and embrace the principles of tax-free living, it helps to look to inspiring stories and quotes for motivation. One such quote is from Warren Buffet: "The best investment you can make is in yourself." Buffet's wealth wasn't built by simply saving money—it was built through smart, tax-efficient investments, the continuous pursuit of knowledge, and a mindset that saw opportunities where others saw obstacles.

Another powerful quote is from Robert Kiyosaki, who said, "Financial freedom is available to those who learn about it and work for it." Financial freedom doesn't happen by accident—it's the result of intentional actions, a shift in mindset, and a commitment to lifelong learning.

Remember, the road to tax-free living isn't just about financial strategies—it's about the mindset that drives those strategies. As you shift the way you think about money and taxes, you unlock the potential to create lasting wealth and true financial freedom. Stay committed to your goals, overcome any obstacles with knowledge and action, and don't be afraid to take control of your financial destiny. Your journey toward tax-free living starts with the belief that it's possible and the mindset to make it a reality.

Developing Habits That Build Lasting Prosperity

Creating lasting prosperity doesn't happen overnight. It's the result of consistent habits and small, intentional actions that compound over time. The habits you develop today will directly influence your financial future, and in the pursuit of tax-free living, these habits are crucial. Developing the right mindset is one thing, but it's the daily practices and choices that truly build wealth. Successful individuals, particularly those who build lasting prosperity, cultivate habits that not only ensure financial growth but also minimize their tax burdens, all while maintaining a healthy balance between enjoying the present and preparing for the future.

One of the most important habits is making saving and investing a regular, non-negotiable part of your life. Whether you're contributing to a retirement account, investing in taxable assets, or funding tax-advantaged vehicles like Roth IRAs or 529 plans, setting aside money for your future should always be a priority. The earlier you start, the more powerful the effects of compound interest become.

That's why automating your savings is so crucial—when the process becomes effortless, it's easier to stick to the habit. Successful individuals understand that prosperity is built through consistency, and they don't let their spending habits undermine their future wealth.

In addition to regular savings, smart investing is another habit that wealth-building individuals master. This doesn't just mean buying stocks or bonds; it means investing with a long-term view and understanding the tax implications of each investment. For example, investing in real estate can provide both income and capital appreciation, but it also offers tax benefits, such as deductions for depreciation and mortgage interest. Having a diverse investment portfolio that maximizes tax-advantaged growth while considering tax-efficient withdrawals is a hallmark of those who understand lasting prosperity.

Tax planning is also an ongoing habit that successful people incorporate into their financial strategy. Rather than thinking about taxes only at the end of the year during tax season, wealthy individuals plan for taxes year-round. This includes maximizing contributions to retirement plans, taking advantage of tax credits, and being mindful of the tax implications of selling assets. Staying ahead of tax laws and adjustments can make a significant difference in how much wealth is retained and how quickly it grows. Regularly reviewing your tax situation with a trusted advisor helps prevent missed opportunities.

Building good financial habits also requires self-discipline. It's easy to fall into the trap of spending money on short-term pleasures, especially in a consumer-driven society. However, individuals who are truly building lasting prosperity know how to balance enjoying life today with setting themselves up for a better tomorrow. The discipline to delay gratification and make thoughtful, intentional choices regarding spending, saving, and investing is a common trait of those who attain long-term wealth.

Staying Motivated on Your Financial Path

Achieving financial freedom is not an easy path. Along the way, there will be challenges, setbacks, and temptations to give up. Staying motivated is essential to making your financial goals a reality, and one of the most important things to understand is that financial success is a marathon, not a sprint. The key to maintaining motivation is to break your larger goals into smaller, more manageable steps and celebrate every milestone along the way.

Start by setting clear, specific, and realistic goals that are tied to your long-term vision. This isn't just about saying "I want to retire early" or "I want to build wealth." It's about breaking that down into actionable goals such as "I will contribute $500 every month to my Roth IRA" or "I will pay off $5,000 in debt by the end of the year." By making your goals measurable, you create a roadmap that allows you to track progress and stay motivated. The small wins you experience along the way will give you the momentum to keep moving forward, especially when you encounter obstacles.

A powerful strategy for maintaining motivation is focusing on the “why” behind your goals. Why do you want to achieve financial freedom? For some, it’s the ability to retire early and travel the world; for others, it’s the desire to provide a better life for their children or break free from the stress of living paycheck to paycheck. Your “why” is what will keep you going on the days when things seem difficult or when you’re tempted to deviate from your path. Reconnecting with your purpose regularly will reignite your passion and determination to stay on course.

It’s also crucial to surround yourself with a supportive network. Whether it’s a spouse, a group of friends, or an online community, having people who understand your goals and support your journey can make all the difference. This network not only provides encouragement but also accountability. When you share your goals with others, you’re more likely to follow through, especially when you have someone to celebrate your successes with.

The journey to financial freedom is filled with ups and downs, and sometimes it’s easy to feel like you’re not making progress fast enough. During these times, it's helpful to look back and reflect on how far you've come. Progress may feel slow at times, but when you compare where you are now to where you started, you'll often find that you've accomplished more than you give yourself credit for.

To keep your motivation strong, learn from the stories of others who have walked the path before you. One such story is that of Warren Buffett, one of the world's wealthiest individuals, who once said, "The best thing you can do is own a business, which you do through your investments, that allows you to stay focused, take your time, and not be forced into making decisions that are driven by short-term thinking." His commitment to long-term investing and patience is a key part of his financial success, and it serves as a powerful reminder that wealth is built over time, through consistent action and a long-term vision.

By adopting a mindset that is focused on discipline, perseverance, and long-term rewards, you can stay motivated and continue moving forward in your financial journey. Set clear goals, stay connected to your purpose, surround yourself with supportive people, and remember that every small step counts. With these strategies, you will not only achieve financial freedom but also enjoy the process of building lasting prosperity.

Conclusion

As you close the final pages of Mastering the Tax-Free Living, remember that achieving financial freedom is a journey—one that requires discipline, strategic thinking, and the right mindset. By now, you've learned the tools, strategies, and approaches that will allow you to reduce your tax burdens, grow your wealth, and take control of your financial future.

But the real power lies in your ability to take action. This book has given you the roadmap, but it's up to you to put these strategies into practice. Whether you're making your first tax-advantage contribution, investing in real estate, or exploring new ways to minimize taxes, every decision you make will bring you closer to a life of financial independence and freedom.

Remember, the path to tax-free living isn't about avoiding taxes—it's about making the tax system work for you. It's about creating a strategy that not only maximizes your wealth but also aligns with your long-term goals.

Keep this book as a resource, revisit its strategies regularly, and stay committed to your financial growth. The wealth and freedom you're striving for are within reach, and by applying the knowledge you've gained here, you'll be well on your way to building a future of financial security and success.

Thank you for taking the first step toward mastering your taxes and achieving financial freedom. Your journey starts now.

About The Author

Andy E. Long is an avid coin collector, historian, and numismatic enthusiast with over two decades of experience in the world of coin collecting. His passion for coins began in his early years, sparked by the stories behind ancient and rare pieces that connected him to different times, cultures, and events. With a keen eye for detail and a profound respect for history, Andy has dedicated himself to understanding the artistry, rarity, and legacy of coins from around the globe.

Throughout his collecting journey, Andy has built a reputation for his thorough knowledge of coin grading, identification, and valuation. He has authored numerous articles on coin collecting, sharing his insights with readers of all levels—from beginners eager to start their collections to seasoned collectors looking to refine their expertise. Andy's approach is rooted in a genuine love for the craft and a desire to make numismatics accessible and enjoyable for everyone.

Beyond his writing, Andy is an active member of several numismatic organizations and frequently attends coin shows and auctions, always on the lookout for unique pieces and opportunities to connect with other collectors. His goal with this book is to provide readers with practical guidance, reliable resources, and the encouragement needed to embark on or deepen their own collecting journeys.

Andy currently resides in the Pacific Northwest, where he continues to build his collection, document his findings, and share his knowledge with a growing community of collectors. When he's not immersed in coins, he enjoys exploring museums, reading about world history, and spending time with his family, who share his enthusiasm for preserving the past through treasured collections.

www.ingramcontent.com/pod-product-compliance
Lightning Source LLC
Chambersburg PA
CBHW071502220526
45472CB00003B/889
* 9 7 9 8 3 0 0 7 2 0 1 9 3 *